Oracle 19c Data Guard

ARUN KUMAR

Oracle 19c Data Guard

Founder and Instructor at DBA Genesis


```
Note: All the queries in this book will look like this format.
```

For any queries, write to support@dbagenesis.com

DEDICATION

I would like to dedicate this book to my family, who has been always there for me whenever I need

ACKNOWLEDGEMENT

Your comments encourage us to produce quality content, please take a second and say 'Hi' to me and let me and my team know what you thought of the book ... p.s. It would mean the world to me if you send a quick email to me ;)

Email: support@dbagenesis.com

- Link to full course: https://dbagenesis.com/
- Link to all DBA courses: https://dbagenesis.com/courses
- Link to support articles: https://support.dbagenesis.com

All the best and I hope you enjoy this book!

Arun Kumar

Table of Content

CHAPTER 1

Data Guard Overview

In Data Guard, we always have a standby server, like Primary and Standby servers. With Oracle, they created multiple types of standby servers. There are basically four types of standby that we can create:

1. Physical Standby
2. Active Data Guard
3. Snapshot Standby
4. Logical Standyby

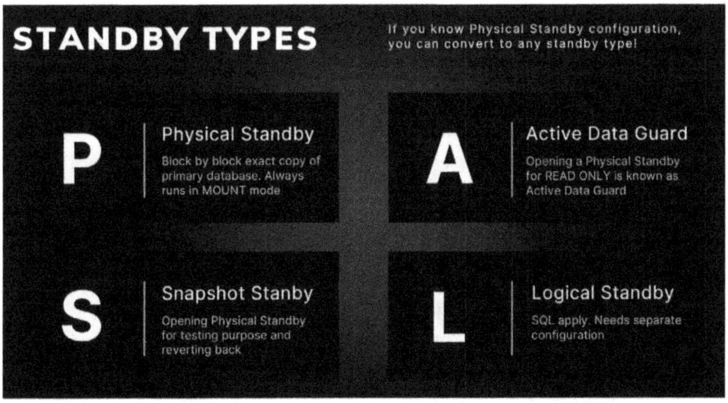
STANDBY TYPES
If you know Physical Standby configuration, you can convert to any standby type!
P
Physical Standby
Block by block exact copy of primary database. Always runs in MOUNT mode
A
Active Data Guard
Opening a Physical Standby for READ ONLY is known as Active Data Guard
S
Snapshot Stanby
Opening Physical Standby for testing purpose and reverting back
L
Logical Standby
SQL apply. Needs separate configuration

If we know the Physical Standby configuration, we can convert it to any standby type. To set up any standby, we first need to configure the Physical Standby and then convert it to the desired standby. Technically, Active Data Guard, Snapshot Standby, and Logical Standby are the byproducts of Physical Standby.

The Physical Standby is like a copy of your primary database, and it is an exact block-by-block replica. Everything that comes from the primary database is replicated or recreated on the Physical Standby. If the primary crashes, the Physical Standby should look like an exact copy of the primary database. Physical Standby always runs in MOUNT mode.

If we open a Physical Standby for READ ONLY is known as Active Data Guard.

If we open a Physical Standby for testing purposes and then revert it back, it is known as Snapshot Standby.

Logical Standby is an open database where we can run only SQL commands. The exact SQL commands that we run on the primary database can also be run on the Logical Standby. However, Logical Standby requires a separate configuration.

Architecture

In the Standby Architecture, we have a primary database and LNS (Log Network Service) acting as a new archive log destination. On the primary database, we have redo log files and an archive destination. There is one specific destination on the primary database where our archive logs are written down.

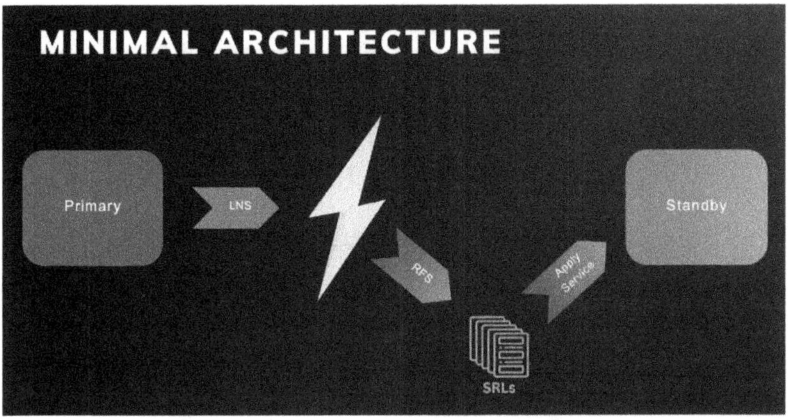

In Oracle, we can have multiple file destinations. We enable a secondary archive destination, which is on a standby server. On the primary database, we specify that archive destination1 should be the local server and archive destination2 should be on a remote server. This way, archive destination2 is enabled, and the background process responsible for sending the archive data from the primary server to the standby server is LNS (Log Network Service). LNS will write the logs from the primary to the standby server.

There is a network connection between the LNS and RFS that we set up using TNS and Listener. This connection is essential because our primary and standby databases operate through the Oracle Listener and TNS connection.

On the standby server, the RFS (Remote File Server) process is responsible for accepting the data coming from the LNS. The LNS process sends the redo data, and RFS reads it on the standby side and writes it to a new type of log file known as standby redo log files.

In one database, we have redo log files and archive log files, but in Data Guard configuration, we have another type of log file which are known as standby log files. The RFS process will write to the standby redo log files and from SRLs log files there is another service which is called as Apply Service (MRP). The Apply Service will read from SRLs and apply the transactions on to standby.

Technically, on the primary database, whatever redo is being generated is transported to a new destination, archive destination2, which points to the standby server. Whenever the primary generates redo and the archive processes are archiving, archive destination2 involves a background process known as LNS. LNS transfers the redo entries over the network. On the standby server, RFS receives these entries and writes them to special log files known as Standby Redo Logs (SRLs). From SRLs, the Apply Service picks up these transactions and starts applying them to the standby database.

Imagine we create a table on primary and we insert some records, and there are a lot of redo and archives that are generated. We did not commit the transaction on primary. Do you think it will still be transferred to standby?

Everythings works with redo. When a user issues commands, and the log file is already archived on the local server, archive destination2, invoked via LNS (Log Network Service), will automatically transfer it. As a result, commands such as `CREATE TABLE` and `INSERT` are applied on the standby database as well. Future commits from the primary will also be transferred to the standby, and if the user rolls back, that rollback will be transferred too. This ensures that the primary and standby databases are in sync and that the standby behaves exactly like the primary, functioning as if it were a standalone database.

If something is done on the primary database, whether committed or not, the standby database does not wait exclusively for committed transactions. The standby operates as a block-by-block copy. Any transaction that runs on the primary, resulting in an archive log being generated, will be transferred to the standby database. This ensures that the standby database remains an accurate and up-to-date replica of the primary database, capturing all changes regardless of their commit status.

When new archive logs are generated on the primary database, LNS will transfer them to the standby server. The RFS on the standby server will receive these logs. They are written to the Standby Redo Logs (SRLs). The Apply Service will then read from the SRLs and execute the transactions against the standby database.

Do you think the standby redo log files name is SRL. Do we need to create this SRL only on standby or both standby and primary server?

The SRLs needs to be created on both sides because if the standby becomes primary, and the primary becomes standby, so the LNS will get started from the new primary in the reverse direction which means over the network on the new standby, we need to have RFS process which is accepting the data following the reverse direction and RFS always writes to SRLs or standby log files.

When your primary database eventually becomes a standby, it will need the Standby Redo Logs (SRLs). Therefore, it's a good idea to create the SRLs even before you create the standby database. By creating SRLs on your primary database in advance, you ensure that when you clone your primary database, the SRLs will be automatically cloned as well.

Do you think all 3 main processes (LNS, RFS and Apply Services) need to start manually or they are auto started?

Whenever a new archive log is generated, LNS reads and pushes it to the standby. LNS starts automatically. When LNS is pushing data over the network, RFS is ready to receive it, and RFS also starts automatically. However, the Apply Service can start either manually or automatically. In a manual setup of Physical Standby or Data Guard, you need to start the Apply Service yourself. In contrast, if you are using Data Guard Broker, it can detect when the Apply Service is down and will automatically start it for you.

As a DBA, you need to the following things:

1. On primary, you got to set the archive destination2 which sends the archives to the standby.
2. You have to create the SRLs on primary because after cloning the SRLs will automatically be created on standby also.
3. You have to set up the network because you need to have a listener and TNS entries flowing in both directions.
4. You got to clone the primary database to standby. Once the cloning is done, then the new changes will automatically come from primary and it will be applied to the standby.

How should the primary and standby server configurations be set up? Should they have the same or different configurations?

Assume that we have a primary server and the client needs a standby setup. We should simply tell the client to create another server with the same configuration as the primary server.

Do you think the primary and standby should be in the same or different location? If it is a different location then how far?

It should be in the different location on a different continent.

LNS - Logwrite Network Server

Whenever an archive log is generated, LNS is responsible for reading and sending it to the standby. You have to set the TNS and listener entries in both directions. LNS is a background process.

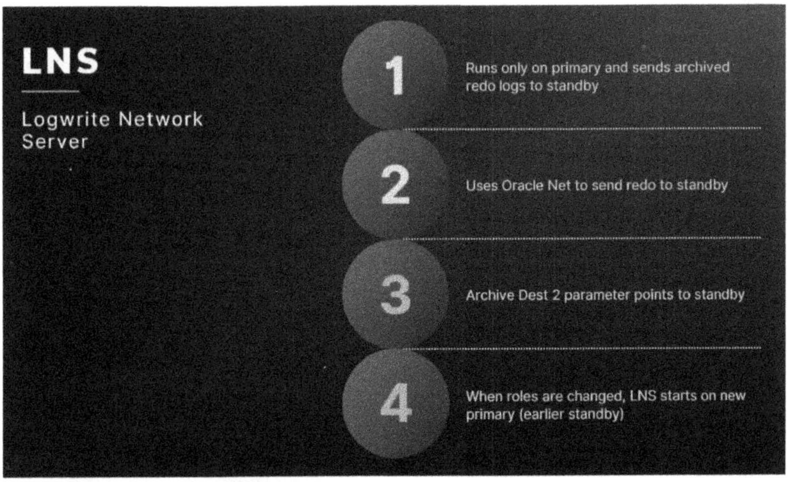
LNS
Logwrite Network Server
1
Runs only on primary and sends archived redo logs to standby
2
Uses Oracle Net to send redo to standby
3
Archive Dest 2 parameter points to standby
4
When roles are changed, LNS starts on new primary (earlier standby)

Do we have to set up the network in the reverse direction or one side is fine?

We have to set up the network in both directions because if the primary becomes standby and the standby becomes primary, we don't want to configure the network during an emergency. It's good to set up the TNS connection from both databases to both sides. Ensure listeners are running on both sides and TNS ping is working from both directions, so that when roles switch, the reverse flow of the logs is smooth.

LNS is a background process, but you have an archive destination2 parameter to set a second destination for your archive logs to flow to the standby. Whenever there is a new archive log, the archive destination2 parameter starts the LNS process. This service reads the archive log and transfers the redo data to the standby.

If stand by becomes primary, LNS will be started over the apply service and it will start pushing the data in the reverse direction

RFS - Remote File Server

Remote File Server (RFS) will run only on standby. The job of RFS is to accept the incoming redo data from the LNS. If standby becomes primary and primary becomes standby then RFS will start accepting the data which is coming in the reverse direction.

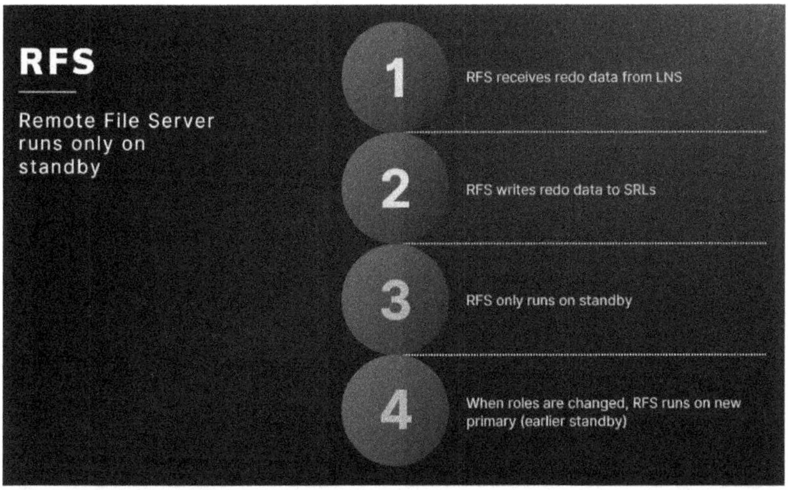

SRL - Standby Redo Logfiles

Standby Redo Logs (SRLs) must be the same size as redo log files because they contain the same redo data. It's a good idea to keep SRLs the same size as your redo log files. SRLs need to be created on the primary as well.

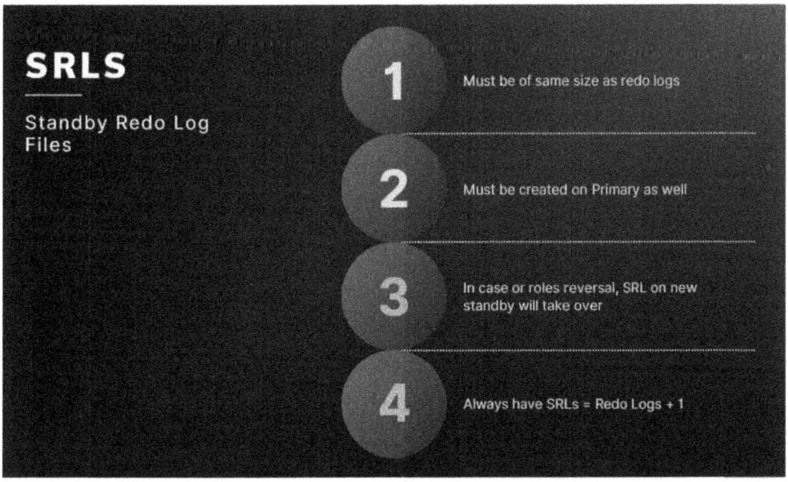

Apply Service

Technically, the background process name is Manage Recovery Process (MRP). It runs on standby because Apply service will read the standby log files and then start to apply the changes.

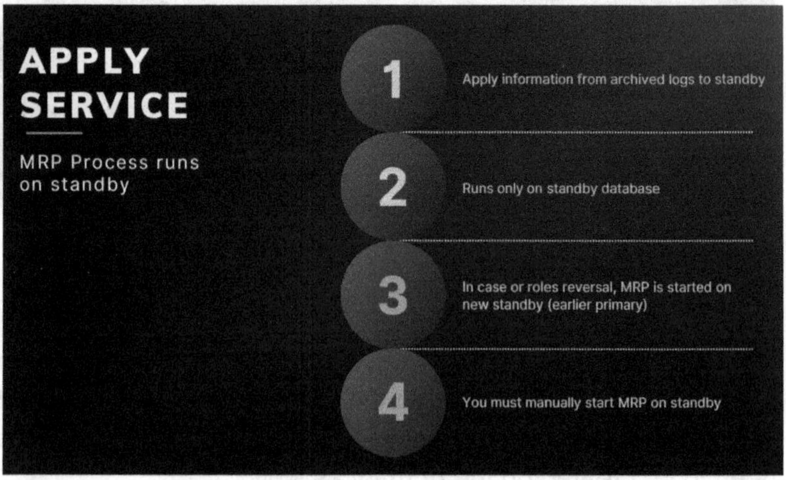

In the primary and standby database, the parameters SID and DB NAME must be the same but DB UNIQUE NAME should be different.

```
PRIMARY:

SID                : E6P
DB NAME            : E6P
DB UNIQUE NAME     : E6P



STANDBY 1:

SID                : E6P
DB NAME            : E6P
DB UNIQUE NAME     : E6P_ST1



================================

STANDBY 2:

SID                : E6P
DB NAME            : E6P
DB UNIQUE NAME     : E6P_ST2
```

How do we know which database in a Data Guard configuration is acting as primary or standby?

In a database configuration with roles like Primary and Standby, each database is assigned only one role. This means that, in a given configuration, only one database can act as the primary, and you can have multiple standby databases. If a standby becomes the primary, the existing primary must be reconfigured to become a standby, as only one primary database can exist in a given configuration.

Assignment

1. What are the best practices for setting up Physical Standby?
2. Can we setup standby with SRLs on Primary?
3. Do we need a license to configure Physical Standby

CHAPTER 2

Physical Standby Setup

We have two server one is [root@ask01 ~]# is our Primary and [root@ask02 ~]# is our standby server and we will install Oracle 19c on Linux on both the servers.

Oracle 19c Installation on Linux:
https://support.dbagenesis.com/post/oracle-19c-installation-on-linux#viewer-dk2h5

Oracle 19c Pre - requisites

Use the YUM repository to perform all the pre-install steps. Make sure your VM is able to ping google.com before executing below command.

```
yum install -y
oracle-database-preinstall-19c
```

[root@aks01 ~]# yum install -y oracle-database-preinstall-19c
Failed to set locale, defaulting to C
ol7_UEKR6 | 3.0 kB 00:00:00
ol7_developer_EPEL | 3.6 kB 00:00:00
ol7_latest | 3.6 kB 00:00:00
ol7_optional_latest | 3.0 kB 00:00:00
(1/4): ol7_latest/x86_64/updateinfo | 3.6 MB 00:00:00
(2/4): ol7_optional_latest/x86_64/updateinfo | 1.5 MB 00:00:00
(3/4): ol7_optional_latest/x86_64/primary_db | 6.3 MB 00:00:00
(4/4): ol7_latest/x86_64/primary_db | 51 MB 00:00:00

Create Oracle home directory and give ownership to Oracle user

```
mkdir -p
/u01/app/oracle/product/19.3/db_home
chown -R oracle:oinstall /u01
chmod -R 775 /u01
```

```
[root@aks01 ~]# mkdir -p /u01/app/oracle/product/19.3/db_home
[root@aks01 ~]# chown -R oracle:oinstall /u01
[root@aks01 ~]# chmod -R 775 /u01
[root@aks01 ~]#
```

```
[root@aks02 ~]# mkdir -p /u01/app/oracle/product/19.3/db_home
[root@aks02 ~]# chown -R oracle:oinstall /u01
[root@aks02 ~]# chmod -R 775 /u01
```

Setup Oracle user bash_profile

```
su - oracle
vi .bash_profile
```

User specific environment and startup programs

```
export ORACLE_SID=CDB
export ORACLE_BASE=/u01/app/oracle
export
ORACLE_HOME=/u01/app/oracle/product/19.3/db_
home

PATH=$PATH:$HOME/.local/bin:$ORACLE_HOME/bin
```

```
[root@aks01 ~]# su - oracle
Last failed login: Tue May 21 06:16:36 CEST 2024 from 139.59.77.147 on ssh:notty
There were 60 failed login attempts since the last successful login.
[oracle@aks01 ~]$ vi .bash_profile
```

```
# .bash_profile

# Get the aliases and functions
if [ -f ~/.bashrc ]; then
        . ~/.bashrc
fi

# User specific environment and startup programs

export ORACLE_SID=CDB
export ORACLE_BASE=/u01/app/oracle
export ORACLE_HOME=/u01/app/oracle/product/19.3/db_home

PATH=$PATH:$HOME/.local/bin:$ORACLE_HOME/bin

export PATH
~
~
~
~
~
~
~
~
~
~
~
~
~
~
~
~
~
~
~
~
~
:wq!
```

```
[oracle@aks01 ~]$ env|grep ORA
ORACLE_SID=CDB
ORACLE_BASE=/u01/app/oracle
ORACLE_HOME=/u01/app/oracle/product/19.3/db_home
[oracle@aks01 ~]$
```

```
[root@aks02 ~]# su - oracle
Last failed login: Tue May 21 11:13:58 CEST 2024 from c83-248-185-188.bredband.tele2.se on ssh:notty
There were 12 failed login attempts since the last successful login.
[oracle@aks02 ~]$
```

```
# .bash_profile

# Get the aliases and functions
if [ -f ~/.bashrc ]; then
        . ~/.bashrc
fi

# User specific environment and startup programs

export ORACLE_SID=CDB
export ORACLE_BASE=/u01/app/oracle
export ORACLE_HOME=/u01/app/oracle/product/19.3/db_home

PATH=$PATH:$HOME/.local/bin:$ORACLE_HOME/bin

export PATH
~
~
~
~
~
~
~
~
~
~
~
~
~
~
~
~
~
~
~
~
~
:wq!
```

```
[oracle@aks02 ~]$ env|grep ORA
ORACLE_SID=CDB
ORACLE_BASE=/u01/app/oracle
ORACLE_HOME=/u01/app/oracle/product/19.3/db_home
[oracle@aks02 ~]$
```

Now install Oracle 19c Software:
https://www.oracle.com/in/database/technologies/oracle-database-software-downloads.html

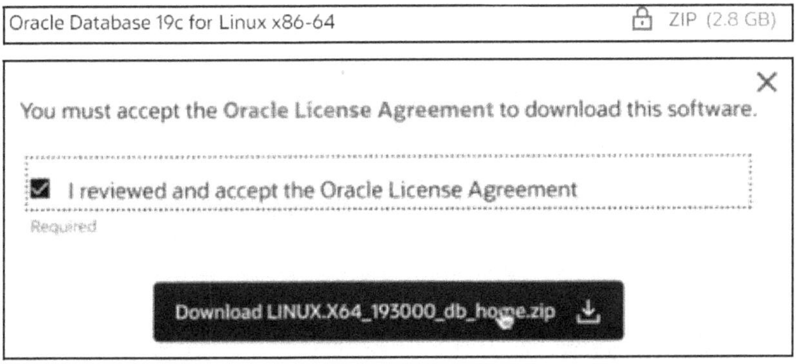

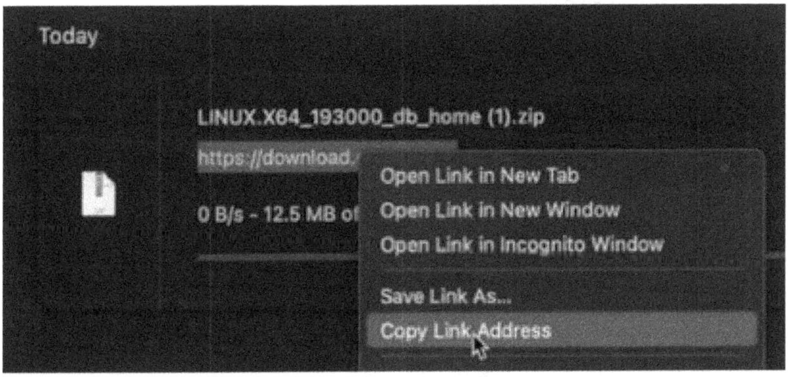

Now let us start downloading the software from Oracle website directly on the primary server

```
Cd $ORACLE_HOME
wget + past the link + -O LINUX.X64_193000_db_home.zip

ls -lrt
unzip LINUX.X64_193000_db_home.zip

ls
df -h

./runInstaller -ignorePrereq -waitforcompletion -silent
\
-responseFile ${ORACLE_HOME}/install/response/db_install.rsp
\
oracle.install.option=INSTALL_DB_SWONLY
\
ORACLE_HOSTNAME=${HOSTNAME}
\
UNIX_GROUP_NAME=oinstall
\
INVENTORY_LOCATION=/u01/app/oraInventory
\
SELECTED_LANGUAGES=en,en_GB
\
ORACLE_HOME=${ORACLE_HOME}
\
ORACLE_BASE=${ORACLE_BASE}
\
oracle.install.db.InstallEdition=EE
\
oracle.install.db.OSDBA_GROUP=dba
\
oracle.install.db.OSBACKUPDBA_GROUP=dba
\
oracle.install.db.OSDGDBA_GROUP=dba
\
oracle.install.db.OSKMDBA_GROUP=dba
\
oracle.install.db.OSRACDBA_GROUP=dba
\
SECURITY_UPDATES_VIA_MYORACLESUPPORT=false
\
DECLINE_SECURITY_UPDATES=true
```

```
[oracle@aks01 db_home]$ wget https://download.oracle.com/otn/linux/oracle19c/190000/LINUX.X64_193000_db_home.zip?AuthParam
=1716288956_0871bd5aeb593fb7de9347269f1e6be7 -O LINUX.X64_193000_db_home.zip
--2024-05-21 12:54:42--  https://download.oracle.com/otn/linux/oracle19c/190000/LINUX.X64_193000_db_home.zip?AuthParam=171
6288956_0871bd5aeb593fb7de9347269f1e6be7
Resolving download.oracle.com (download.oracle.com)... 184.50.200.91
Connecting to download.oracle.com (download.oracle.com)|184.50.200.91|:443... connected.
HTTP request sent, awaiting response... 200 OK
Length: 3059705302 (2.8G) [application/zip]
Saving to: 'LINUX.X64_193000_db_home.zip'

100%[===========================================================================>] 3,059,705,302  180MB/s   in 16s

2024-05-21 12:54:59 (185 MB/s) - 'LINUX.X64_193000_db_home.zip' saved [3059705302/3059705302]

[oracle@aks01 db_home]$
[oracle@aks01 db_home]$
[oracle@aks01 db_home]$
[oracle@aks01 db_home]$
[oracle@aks01 db_home]$ ls -lrt
total 2988000
-rw-r--r-- 1 oracle oinstall 3059705302 Apr 24  2019 LINUX.X64_193000_db_home.zip
[oracle@aks01 db_home]$
[oracle@aks01 db_home]$
[oracle@aks01 db_home]$ unzip LINUX.X64_193000_db_home.zip
```

```
[oracle@aks01 db_home]$ ls
addnode     data         env.ora        jlib                          olap     perl      root.sh.old      sqlplus
apex        dbjava       has            ldap                          OPatch   plsql     root.sh.old.1    srvm
assistants  dbs          hs             lib                           opmn     precomp   runInstaller     suptools
bin         deinstall    install        LINUX.X64_193000_db_home.zip  oracore  QOpatch   schagent.conf    ucp
clone       demo         instantclient  md                            ord      R         sdk              usm
crs         diagnostics  inventory      mgw                           ords     racg      slax             utl
css         dmu          javavm         network                       oss      rdbms     sqldeveloper     wwg
ctx         drdaas       jdbc           nls                           oui      relnotes  sqlj             xdk
cv          dv           jdk            odbc                          owm      root.sh   sqlpatch
[oracle@aks01 db_home]$
[oracle@aks01 db_home]$
[oracle@aks01 db_home]$ df -h
Filesystem      Size  Used Avail Use% Mounted on
devtmpfs        1.7G     0  1.7G   0% /dev
tmpfs           1.8G     0  1.8G   0% /dev/shm
tmpfs           1.8G  580K  1.8G   1% /run
tmpfs           1.8G     0  1.8G   0% /sys/fs/cgroup
/dev/sda3        67G   13G   52G  20% /
/dev/sda1       974M  344M  564M  38% /boot
tmpfs           354M     0  354M   0% /run/user/0
[oracle@aks01 db_home]$
```

```
[oracle@aks01 db_home]$
[oracle@aks01 db_home]$ ./runInstaller -ignorePrereq -waitforcompletion -silent      \
> -responseFile ${ORACLE_HOME}/install/response/db_install.rsp \
> oracle.install.option=INSTALL_DB_SWONLY                       \
> ORACLE_HOSTNAME=${HOSTNAME}                                   \
> UNIX_GROUP_NAME=oinstall                                      \
> INVENTORY_LOCATION=/u01/app/oraInventory                      \
> SELECTED_LANGUAGES=en,en_GB                                   \
> ORACLE_HOME=${ORACLE_HOME}                                    \
> ORACLE_BASE=${ORACLE_BASE}                                    \
> oracle.install.db.InstallEdition=EE                           \
> oracle.install.db.OSDBA_GROUP=dba                             \
> oracle.install.db.OSBACKUPDBA_GROUP=dba                       \
> oracle.install.db.OSDGDBA_GROUP=dba                           \
> oracle.install.db.OSKMDBA_GROUP=dba                           \
> oracle.install.db.OSRACDBA_GROUP=dba                          \
> SECURITY_UPDATES_VIA_MYORACLESUPPORT=false                    \
> DECLINE_SECURITY_UPDATES=true
Launching Oracle Database Setup Wizard...
```

```
[oracle@aks01 db_home]$
[oracle@aks01 db_home]$ exit
logout
[root@aks01 ~]#
[root@aks01 ~]#
[root@aks01 ~]# /u01/app/oraInventory/orainstRoot.sh
Changing permissions of /u01/app/oraInventory.
Adding read,write permissions for group.
Removing read,write,execute permissions for world.

Changing groupname of /u01/app/oraInventory to oinstall.
The execution of the script is complete.
[root@aks01 ~]#
[root@aks01 ~]#
[root@aks01 ~]# /u01/app/oracle/product/19.3/db_home/root.sh
Check /u01/app/oracle/product/19.3/db_home/install/root_aks01.dbageneis.com_2024-05-21_12-59-48-612377946.log for the outp
ut of root script
[root@aks01 ~]#
[root@aks01 ~]#
[root@aks01 ~]#
```

```
[oracle@aks02 db_home]$
[oracle@aks02 db_home]$ wget https://download.oracle.com/otn/linux/oracle19c/190000/LINUX.X64_193000_db_home.zip?AuthParam
=1716288956_0871bd5aeb593fb7de9347269f1e6be7 -O LINUX.X64_193000_db_home.zip
--2024-05-21 12:55:03--  https://download.oracle.com/otn/linux/oracle19c/190000/LINUX.X64_193000_db_home.zip?AuthParam=171
6288956_0871bd5aeb593fb7de9347269f1e6be7
Resolving download.oracle.com (download.oracle.com)... 184.50.200.91
Connecting to download.oracle.com (download.oracle.com)|184.50.200.91|:443... connected.
HTTP request sent, awaiting response... 200 OK
Length: 3059705302 (2.8G) [application/zip]
Saving to: 'LINUX.X64_193000_db_home.zip'

100%[===========================================================================>] 3,059,705,302  313MB/s   in 10s

2024-05-21 12:55:13 (287 MB/s) - 'LINUX.X64_193000_db_home.zip' saved [3059705302/3059705302]

[oracle@aks02 db_home]$
[oracle@aks02 db_home]$
[oracle@aks02 db_home]$
[oracle@aks02 db_home]$ ls -lrt
total 2988000
-rw-r--r-- 1 oracle oinstall 3059705302 Apr 24  2019 LINUX.X64_193000_db_home.zip
[oracle@aks02 db_home]$
[oracle@aks02 db_home]$
[oracle@aks02 db_home]$
[oracle@aks02 db_home]$ unzip LINUX.X64_193000_db_home.zip
```

```
[oracle@aks02 db_home]$ ls
addnode     data         env.ora        jlib                         olap     perl      root.sh.old     sqlplus
apex        dbjava       has            ldap                         OPatch   plsql     root.sh.old.1   srvm
assistants  dbs          hs             lib                          opmn     precomp   runInstaller    suptools
bin         deinstall    install        LINUX.X64_193000_db_home.zip oracore  QOpatch   schagent.conf   ucp
clone       demo         instantclient  md                           ord      R         sdk             usm
crs         diagnostics  inventory      mgw                          ords     racg      slax            utl
css         dmu          javavm         network                      oss      rdbms     sqldeveloper    wwg
ctx         drdaas       jdbc           nls                          oui      relnotes  sqlj            xdk
cv          dv           jdk            odbc                         owm      root.sh   sqlpatch
[oracle@aks02 db_home]$
```

```
[oracle@aks02 db_home]$ ./runInstaller -ignorePrereq -waitforcompletion -silent        \
> -responseFile ${ORACLE_HOME}/install/response/db_install.rsp \
> oracle.install.option=INSTALL_DB_SWONLY                       \
> ORACLE_HOSTNAME=${HOSTNAME}                                   \
> UNIX_GROUP_NAME=oinstall                                      \
> INVENTORY_LOCATION=/u01/app/oraInventory                      \
> SELECTED_LANGUAGES=en,en_GB                                   \
> ORACLE_HOME=${ORACLE_HOME}                                    \
> ORACLE_BASE=${ORACLE_BASE}                                    \
> oracle.install.db.InstallEdition=EE                           \
> oracle.install.db.OSDBA_GROUP=dba                             \
> oracle.install.db.OSBACKUPDBA_GROUP=dba                       \
> oracle.install.db.OSDGDBA_GROUP=dba                           \
> oracle.install.db.OSKMDBA_GROUP=dba                           \
> oracle.install.db.OSRACDBA_GROUP=dba                          \
> SECURITY_UPDATES_VIA_MYORACLESUPPORT=false                    \
> DECLINE_SECURITY_UPDATES=true

Launching Oracle Database Setup Wizard...
```

```
[oracle@aks02 db_home]$
[oracle@aks02 db_home]$ exit
logout
[root@aks02 ~]#
[root@aks02 ~]# /u01/app/oraInventory/orainstRoot.sh
Changing permissions of /u01/app/oraInventory.
Adding read,write permissions for group.
Removing read,write,execute permissions for world.

Changing groupname of /u01/app/oraInventory to oinstall.
The execution of the script is complete.
[root@aks02 ~]#
[root@aks02 ~]# /u01/app/oracle/product/19.3/db_home/root.sh
Check /u01/app/oracle/product/19.3/db_home/install/root_aks02.dbagenesis.com_2024-05-21_13-00-05-923419544.log for the outp
ut of root script
[root@aks02 ~]#
```

DBCA Create 19c Container Database

To create 19c container database along with multiple PDBs, use below

```
dbca -silent -createDatabase                                   \
     -templateName General_Purpose.dbc                         \
     -gdbname ${ORACLE_SID} -sid  ${ORACLE_SID}                \
     -characterSet AL32UTF8                                    \
     -sysPassword enterCDB#123                                 \
     -systemPassword enterCDB#123                              \
     -createAsContainerDatabase true                           \
     -totalMemory 2000                                         \
     -storageType FS                                           \
     -datafileDestination /u01/${ORACLE_SID}                   \
     -emConfiguration NONE                                     \
     -numberOfPDBs 2                                           \
     -pdbName PDB                                              \
     -pdbAdminPassword enterPDB#123                            \
     -ignorePreReqs
```

Check all the containers inside the database

```
sqlplus / as sysdba
SELECT  NAME, OPEN_MODE, CDB FROM
V$DATABASE;
SELECT CON_ID, NAME, OPEN_MODE FROM
V$CONTAINERS;
```

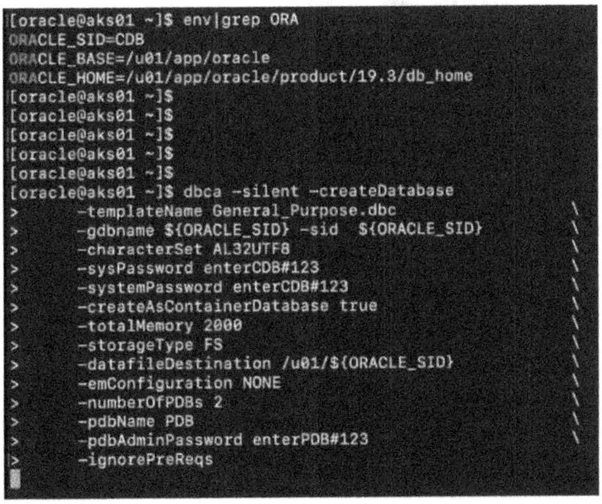

Oracle Data Guard Physical Standby Configuration:
https://support.dbagenesis.com/post/oracle-data-guard-physical-standby-configuration

Primary database changes

Primary must run in archive log mode. Check the archive log mode

```
SELECT log_mode FROM v$database;

LOG_MODE
------------
NOARCHIVELOG
```

If it is not running in archive log mode, then enable it

```
SQL> shutdown immediate
SQL> startup mount
SQL> alter database archivelog;
SQL> alter database open;
SQL> archive log list;
```

Enable force logging on primary: In oracle, users can restrict redo generation for SQL by using NOLOGGING clause. This NOLOGGING transaction will be a problem for physical standby. Hence, we force logging so even if user uses NOLOGGING clause, every SQL will be logged on to redo

```
SQL> alter database force logging;
SQL> select name, force_logging from
v$database;
```

```
[oracle@aks01 ~]$ ps -ef|grep pmon
oracle   13085     1  0 13:15 ?        00:00:00 ora_pmon_CDB
oracle   13914 13889  0 13:23 pts/1    00:00:00 grep --color=auto pmon
[oracle@aks01 ~]$
[oracle@aks01 ~]$
[oracle@aks01 ~]$
[oracle@aks01 ~]$
[oracle@aks01 ~]$ env|grep ORA
ORACLE_SID=CDB
ORACLE_BASE=/u01/app/oracle
ORACLE_HOME=/u01/app/oracle/product/19.3/db_home
[oracle@aks01 ~]$
```

```
[oracle@aks01 ~]$ sqlplus / as sysdba

SQL*Plus: Release 19.0.0.0.0 - Production on Tue May 21 13:25:08 2024
Version 19.3.0.0.0

Copyright (c) 1982, 2019, Oracle.  All rights reserved.


Connected to:
Oracle Database 19c Enterprise Edition Release 19.0.0.0.0 - Production
Version 19.3.0.0.0

SQL>
SQL> shut immediate;
Database closed.
Database dismounted.
ORACLE instance shut down.
SQL>
SQL>
SQL> startup mount;
ORACLE instance started.

Total System Global Area 1577055360 bytes
Fixed Size                  9135232 bytes
Variable Size             385875968 bytes
Database Buffers         1174405120 bytes
Redo Buffers                7639040 bytes
Database mounted.
SQL>
```

```
SQL> alter database archivelog;

Database altered.

SQL>
SQL>
SQL> alter database open;

Database altered.

SQL>
SQL>
SQL> archive log list;
Database log mode              Archive Mode
Automatic archival             Enabled
Archive destination            /u01/app/oracle/product/19.3/db_home/dbs/arch
Oldest online log sequence     5
Next log sequence to archive   7
Current log sequence           7
SQL>
SQL>
SQL>
SQL> alter database force logging;

Database altered.

SQL>
SQL>
SQL> select name, force_logging from v$database;

NAME      FORCE_LOGGING
--------- ---------------------------------------
CDB       YES
```

Standby file management: We need to make sure whenever we add/drop datafile in primary database, those files are also added / dropped on standby

```
SQL> alter system set
standby_file_management = 'AUTO';
```

```
SQL> alter system set standby_file_management = 'AUTO';

System altered.

SQL>
```

Create standby log files: You must create standby log files on primary. These files are used by a standby database to store redo it receives from the primary database.

Our primary may become standby later and we would need them, so better to create it. First check the current log groups

```
SQL> select GROUP#, THREAD#,
bytes/1024/1024, MEMBERS, STATUS from v$log;

SQL> select member from v$logfile;
```

```
SQL> select GROUP#, THREAD#, bytes/1024/1024, MEMBERS, STATUS from v$log;

    GROUP#    THREAD# BYTES/1024/1024    MEMBERS STATUS
---------- ---------- --------------- ---------- ----------------
         1          1             200          1 CURRENT
         2          1             200          1 INACTIVE
         3          1             200          1 INACTIVE

SQL>
SQL>
SQL>
SQL>
SQL>
SQL> select member from v$logfile;

MEMBER
--------------------------------------------------------------------------------
/u01/CDB/redo03.log
/u01/CDB/redo02.log
/u01/CDB/redo01.log

SQL>
```

Add the standby log files, make sure the group number should be from a different series like in this case we choose to start with 11 and above. This helps in easy differentiation.

Make sure that the thread# and the log file size is exactly the same. Oracle also recommends always creating n+1 standby log files. Where n is the total number of log files.

```
ALTER DATABASE ADD STANDBY LOGFILE THREAD 1 GROUP
11 '/u01/CDB/srl01.log' SIZE 200M;
ALTER DATABASE ADD STANDBY LOGFILE THREAD 1 GROUP
11 '/u01/CDB/srl02.log' SIZE 200M;
ALTER DATABASE ADD STANDBY LOGFILE THREAD 1 GROUP
11 '/u01/CDB/srl03.log' SIZE 200M;
ALTER DATABASE ADD STANDBY LOGFILE THREAD 1 GROUP
11 '/u01/CDB/srl04.log' SIZE 200M;
```

```
SQL> ALTER DATABASE ADD STANDBY LOGFILE THREAD 1 GROUP 11 '/u01/CDB/srl01.log' size 200M;

Database altered.

SQL> ALTER DATABASE ADD STANDBY LOGFILE THREAD 1 GROUP 12 '/u01/CDB/srl02.log' size 200M;

Database altered.

SQL> ALTER DATABASE ADD STANDBY LOGFILE THREAD 1 GROUP 13 '/u01/CDB/srl03.log' size 200M;

Database altered.

SQL> ALTER DATABASE ADD STANDBY LOGFILE THREAD 1 GROUP 14 '/u01/CDB/srl04.log' size 200M;

Database altered.

SQL>
```

Check the standby log files via below query

```
SQL> SELECT
GROUP#,THREAD#,SEQUENCE#,ARCHIVED,STATUS
FROM V$STANDBY_LOG;
```

```
SQL> SELECT GROUP#,THREAD#,SEQUENCE#,ARCHIVED,STATUS FROM V$STANDBY_LOG;

    GROUP#    THREAD#  SEQUENCE# ARC STATUS
---------- ---------- ---------- --- ----------
        11          1          0 YES UNASSIGNED
        12          1          0 YES UNASSIGNED
        13          1          0 YES UNASSIGNED
        14          1          0 YES UNASSIGNED
```

Enable flashback on primary: Flashback database is highly recommended because in case of failover, you need not recreate primary database from scratch

```
SQL> alter system set
db_recovery_file_dest_size=45g;
SQL> alter database flashback on;
SQL> select flashback_on from v$database;
```

If flashback parameters are not set properly, use below commands

```
SQL> show parameter recovery;
SQL> alter system set
db_recovery_file_dest_size=20g;
SQL> alter system set
db_recovery_file_dest='/u01/CDB/FRA';

SQL> show parameter db_recovery;
SQL> alter database flashback on;
```

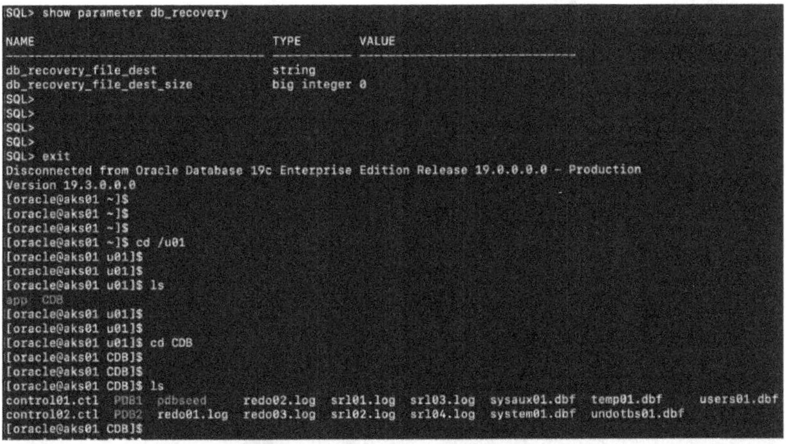

```
SQL> show parameter db_recovery

NAME                                 TYPE        VALUE
------------------------------------ ----------- ------------------------------
db_recovery_file_dest                string
db_recovery_file_dest_size           big integer 0
SQL>
SQL>
SQL>
SQL>
SQL> exit
Disconnected from Oracle Database 19c Enterprise Edition Release 19.0.0.0.0 - Production
Version 19.3.0.0.0
[oracle@aks01 ~]$
[oracle@aks01 ~]$
[oracle@aks01 ~]$
[oracle@aks01 ~]$ cd /u01
[oracle@aks01 u01]$
[oracle@aks01 u01]$
[oracle@aks01 u01]$ ls
app  CDB
[oracle@aks01 u01]$
[oracle@aks01 u01]$
[oracle@aks01 u01]$ cd CDB
[oracle@aks01 CDB]$
[oracle@aks01 CDB]$
[oracle@aks01 CDB]$ ls
control01.ctl  PDB1  pdbseed     redo02.log  srl01.log  srl03.log  sysaux01.dbf  temp01.dbf     users01.dbf
control02.ctl  PDB2  redo01.log  redo03.log  srl02.log  srl04.log  system01.dbf  undotbs01.dbf
[oracle@aks01 CDB]$
```

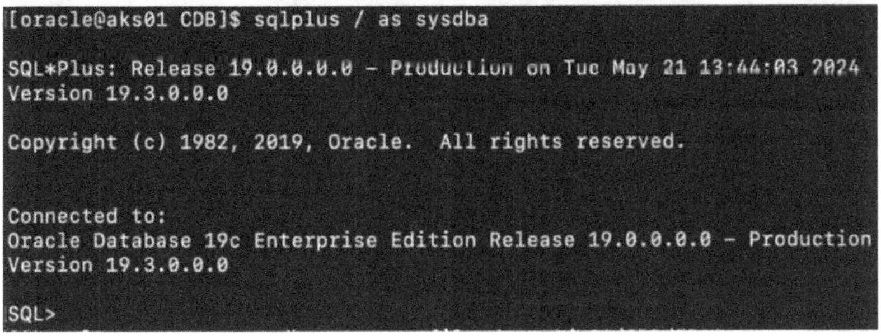

```
[oracle@aks01 CDB]$ sqlplus / as sysdba

SQL*Plus: Release 19.0.0.0.0 - Production on Tue May 21 13:44:03 2024
Version 19.3.0.0.0

Copyright (c) 1982, 2019, Oracle.  All rights reserved.


Connected to:
Oracle Database 19c Enterprise Edition Release 19.0.0.0.0 - Production
Version 19.3.0.0.0

SQL>
```

```
SQL> alter system set db_recovery_file_dest_size=20G;

System altered.

SQL>
SQL>
SQL> alter system set db_recovery_file_dest='/u01/CDB/FRA';

System altered.
```

```
SQL>
SQL> show parameter db_recovery

NAME                                 TYPE        VALUE
------------------------------------ ----------- ------------
db_recovery_file_dest                string      /u01/CDB/FRA
db_recovery_file_dest_size           big integer 20G
SQL>
SQL>
SQL> !df -h
Filesystem      Size  Used Avail Use% Mounted on
devtmpfs        1.7G     0  1.7G   0% /dev
tmpfs           1.8G     0  1.8G   0% /dev/shm
tmpfs           1.8G  612K  1.8G   1% /run
tmpfs           1.8G     0  1.8G   0% /sys/fs/cgroup
/dev/sda3        67G   19G   46G  29% /
/dev/sda1       974M  344M  564M  38% /boot
tmpfs           354M     0  354M   0% /run/user/0

SQL>
SQL> alter database flashback on;

Database altered.
```

Check DB Unique name parameter on primary: Make sure your primary database has DB_UNIQUE_NAME parameter set for consistency. If it's not set properly, use ALTER SYSTEM SET command

```
SQL> show parameter db_unique_name
SQL> show parameter db_name
```

```
SQL> show parameter db_unique

NAME                                 TYPE        VALUE
------------------------------------ ----------- ------------------------------
db_unique_name                       string      CDB
SQL>
SQL>
SQL> show parameter db_name;

NAME                                 TYPE        VALUE
------------------------------------ ----------- ------------------------------
db_name                              string      CDB
SQL>
SQL>
SQL>
SQL>
SQL> exit
Disconnected from Oracle Database 19c Enterprise Edition Release 19.0.0.0.0 - Production
Version 19.3.0.0.0
```

Configure network

Let us configure the network on both the servers.

Use below tns entries and put them under ORACLE user HOME/network/admin/tnsnames.ora. Change host as per your environment and execute on both primary and standby.

Notice the use of the SID, rather than the SERVICE_NAME in the entries. This is important as the broker will need to connect to the databases when they are down, so the services will not be present.

```
vi $ORACLE_HOME/network/admin/tnsnames.ora

CDB =
  (DESCRIPTION =
    (ADDRESS_LIST =
      (ADDRESS = (PROTOCOL = TCP)(HOST =
65.109.170.250)(PORT = 1521))
    )
    (CONNECT_DATA =
      (SID = CDB)
    )
  )

CDB_STB =
  (DESCRIPTION =
    (ADDRESS_LIST =
      (ADDRESS = (PROTOCOL = TCP)(HOST =
95.217.211.31)(PORT = 1521))
    )
    (CONNECT_DATA =
      (SID = CDB)
    )
  )
```

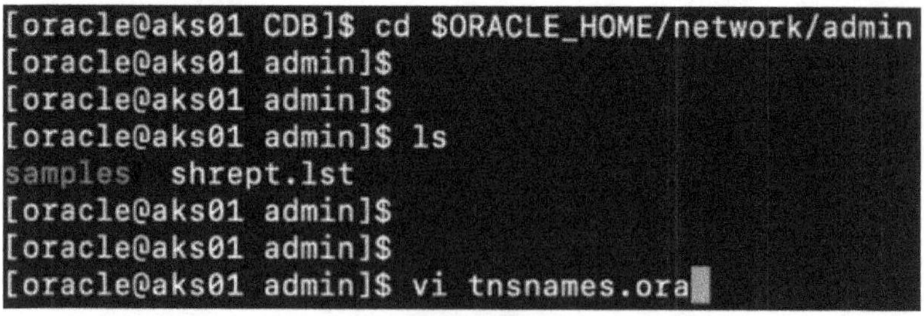

[oracle@aks01 CDB]$ cd $ORACLE_HOME/network/admin
[oracle@aks01 admin]$
[oracle@aks01 admin]$
[oracle@aks01 admin]$ ls
samples shrept.lst
[oracle@aks01 admin]$
[oracle@aks01 admin]$
[oracle@aks01 admin]$ vi tnsnames.ora

```
CDB =
  (DESCRIPTION =
    (ADDRESS_LIST =
      (ADDRESS = (PROTOCOL = TCP)(HOST = 65.109.170.250)(PORT = 1521))
    )
    (CONNECT_DATA =
      (SID = CDB)
    )
  )

CDB_STB =
  (DESCRIPTION =
    (ADDRESS_LIST =
      (ADDRESS = (PROTOCOL = TCP)(HOST = 95.217.211.31)(PORT = 1521))
    )
    (CONNECT_DATA =
      (SID = CDB)
    )
  )
~
~
~
~
~
~
~
~
~
~
~
~
~
~
~
~
~
~
:wq!
```

```
[root@aks02 ~]# su - oracle
Last login: Tue May 21 13:00:05 CEST 2024 on pts/0
[oracle@aks02 ~]$
[oracle@aks02 ~]$
[oracle@aks02 ~]$
[oracle@aks02 ~]$ cd $ORACLE_HOME/network/admin
[oracle@aks02 admin]$
[oracle@aks02 admin]$
[oracle@aks02 admin]$ vi tnsnames.ora
```

```
CDB =
  (DESCRIPTION =
    (ADDRESS_LIST =
      (ADDRESS = (PROTOCOL = TCP)(HOST = 65.109.170.250)(PORT = 1521))
    )
    (CONNECT_DATA =
      (SID = CDB)
    )
  )

CDB_STB =
  (DESCRIPTION =
    (ADDRESS_LIST =
      (ADDRESS = (PROTOCOL = TCP)(HOST = 95.217.211.31)(PORT = 1521))
    )
    (CONNECT_DATA =
      (SID = CDB)
    )
  )
~
~
~
~
~
~
~
~
~
~
~
~
~
~
~
~
~
~
:wq!
```

Configure listener on primary database. Since the broker will need to connect to the database when it's down, we can't rely on auto-registration with the listener, hence the explicit entry for the database.

```
vi listener.ora

LISTENER =
  (DESCRIPTION_LIST =
    (DESCRIPTION =
      (ADDRESS = (PROTOCOL = TCP)(HOST =
65.109.170.250)(PORT = 1521))
    )
  )

SID_LIST_LISTENER =
  (SID_LIST =
    (SID_DESC =
      (GLOBAL_DBNAME = CDB_DGMGRL)
      (ORACLE_HOME =
/u01/app/oracle/product/19.3/db_home)
      (SID_NAME = CDB)
    )
  )

ADR_BASE_LISTENER = /u01/app/oracle
```

```
[oracle@aks01 admin]$ vi listener.ora
[oracle@aks01 admin]$
```

```
LISTENER =
  (DESCRIPTION_LIST =
    (DESCRIPTION =
      (ADDRESS = (PROTOCOL = TCP)(HOST = 65.109.170.250)(PORT = 1521))
    )
  )

SID_LIST_LISTENER =
  (SID_LIST =
    (SID_DESC =
      (GLOBAL_DBNAME = CDB_DGMGRL)
      (ORACLE_HOME = /u01/app/oracle/product/19.3/db_home)
      (SID_NAME = CDB)
    )
  )

ADR_BASE_LISTENER = /u01/app/oracle
~
~
~
~
~
~
~
~
~
~
~
~
~
~
~
~
~
~
~
~
:wq!
```

Configure listener on standby. Since the broker will need to connect to the database when it's down, we can't rely on auto-registration with the listener, hence the explicit entry for the database.

```
vi listener.ora

LISTENER =
  (DESCRIPTION_LIST =
    (DESCRIPTION =
      (ADDRESS = (PROTOCOL = TCP)(HOST =
95.217.211.31)(PORT = 1521))
    )
  )

SID_LIST_LISTENER =
  (SID_LIST =
    (SID_DESC =
      (GLOBAL_DBNAME = CDB_STB_DGMGRL)
      (ORACLE_HOME =
/u01/app/oracle/product/19.3/db_home)
      (SID_NAME = CDB)
    )
  )

ADR_BASE_LISTENER = /u01/app/oracle
```

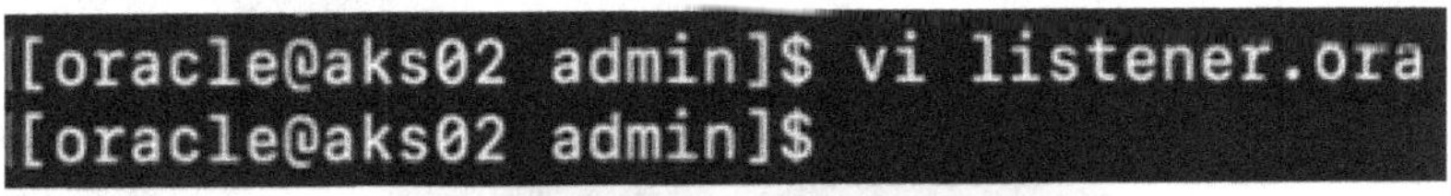

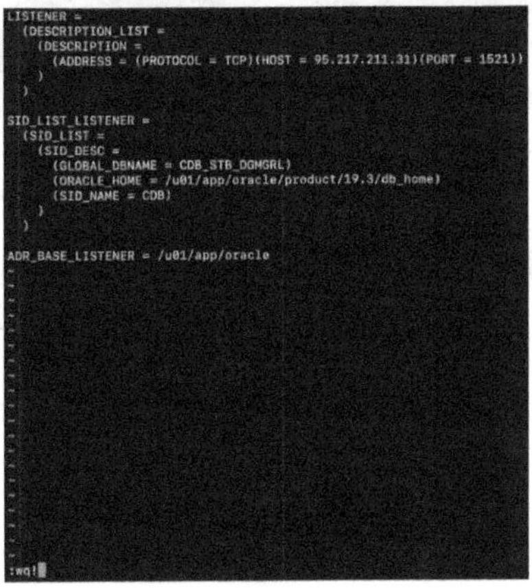

Let us start the listener on both the server

```
lsnrctl start listener
```

```
tnsping cdb
tnsping cdb_stb
```

```
[oracle@aks01 admin]$ lsnrctl start listener

LSNRCTL for Linux: Version 19.0.0.0.0 - Production on 21-MAY-2024 14:01:25

Copyright (c) 1991, 2019, Oracle.  All rights reserved.

Starting /u01/app/oracle/product/19.3/db_home/bin/tnslsnr: please wait...

TNSLSNR for Linux: Version 19.0.0.0.0 - Production
System parameter file is /u01/app/oracle/product/19.3/db_home/network/admin/listener.ora
Log messages written to /u01/app/oracle/diag/tnslsnr/aks01/listener/alert/log.xml
Listening on: (DESCRIPTION=(ADDRESS=(PROTOCOL=tcp)(HOST=65.109.170.250)(PORT=1521)))

Connecting to (DESCRIPTION=(ADDRESS=(PROTOCOL=TCP)(HOST=65.109.170.250)(PORT=1521)))
STATUS of the LISTENER
------------------------
Alias                     listener
Version                   TNSLSNR for Linux: Version 19.0.0.0.0 - Production
Start Date                21-MAY-2024 14:01:26
Uptime                    0 days 0 hr. 0 min. 0 sec
Trace Level               off
Security                  ON: Local OS Authentication
SNMP                      OFF
Listener Parameter File   /u01/app/oracle/product/19.3/db_home/network/admin/listener.ora
Listener Log File         /u01/app/oracle/diag/tnslsnr/aks01/listener/alert/log.xml
Listening Endpoints Summary...
  (DESCRIPTION=(ADDRESS=(PROTOCOL=tcp)(HOST=65.109.170.250)(PORT=1521)))
Services Summary...
Service "CDB_DGMGRL" has 1 instance(s).
  Instance "CDB", status UNKNOWN, has 1 handler(s) for this service...
The command completed successfully
[oracle@aks01 admin]$
```

```
[oracle@aks01 admin]$ tnsping cdb

TNS Ping Utility for Linux: Version 19.0.0.0.0 - Production on 21-MAY-2024 14:01:41

Copyright (c) 1997, 2019, Oracle.  All rights reserved.

Used parameter files:


Used TNSNAMES adapter to resolve the alias
Attempting to contact (DESCRIPTION = (ADDRESS_LIST = (ADDRESS = (PROTOCOL = TCP)(HOST = 65.109.170.250)(PORT = 1521))) (CO
NNECT_DATA = (SID = CDB)))
OK (10 msec)
[oracle@aks01 admin]$
```

```
[oracle@aks01 admin]$ tnsping cdb_stb

TNS Ping Utility for Linux: Version 19.0.0.0.0 - Production on 21-MAY-2024 14:01:49

Copyright (c) 1997, 2019, Oracle.  All rights reserved.

Used parameter files:


Used TNSNAMES adapter to resolve the alias
Attempting to contact (DESCRIPTION = (ADDRESS_LIST = (ADDRESS = (PROTOCOL = TCP)(HOST = 95.217.211.31)(PORT = 1521))) (CON
NECT_DATA = (SID = CDB)))
TNS-12543: TNS:destination host unreachable
[oracle@aks01 admin]$
```

If you get the above error when you run the command `tnsping cdb_stb` which means you need to enable / open 1521 port on the server itself.

Run the below code as root user

```
firewall-cmd --zone=public
--add-port=1521/tcp --permanent
```

```
[oracle@aks01 admin]$ exit
logout
[root@aks01 ~]#
[root@aks01 ~]#
[root@aks01 ~]# firewall-cmd --zone=public --add-port=1521/tcp --permanent
success
[root@aks01 ~]#
```

If it still exists then reload the `firewall firewall-cmd--reload or` reboot the server.

```
[oracle@aks01 ~]$
[oracle@aks01 ~]$ exit
logout
[root@aks01 ~]#
[root@aks01 ~]#
[root@aks01 ~]# firewall-cmd --reload
success
[root@aks01 ~]#
```

```
[root@aks01 ~]# su - oracle
Last login: Tue May 21 14:02:42 CEST 2024 on pts/1
[oracle@aks01 ~]$
[oracle@aks01 ~]$
[oracle@aks01 ~]$
[oracle@aks01 ~]$ tnsping cdb_stb

TNS Ping Utility for Linux: Version 19.0.0.0.0 - Production on 21-MAY-2024 14:03:40

Copyright (c) 1997, 2019, Oracle.  All rights reserved.

Used parameter files:


Used TNSNAMES adapter to resolve the alias
Attempting to contact (DESCRIPTION = (ADDRESS_LIST = (ADDRESS = (PROTOCOL = TCP)(HOST = 95.217.211.31)(PORT = 1521))) (CON
NECT_DATA = (SID = CDB)))
OK (10 msec)
```

Note: Make sure that each server can ping the other. If the ping is not working, it means the network is not set up in both directions, and there's no point in proceeding further.

```
[oracle@aks02 admin]$ lsnrctl start listener

LSNRCTL for Linux: Version 19.0.0.0.0 - Production on 21-MAY-2024 14:01:33

Copyright (c) 1991, 2019, Oracle.  All rights reserved.

Starting /u01/app/oracle/product/19.3/db_home/bin/tnslsnr: please wait...

TNSLSNR for Linux: Version 19.0.0.0.0 - Production
System parameter file is /u01/app/oracle/product/19.3/db_home/network/admin/listener.ora
Log messages written to /u01/app/oracle/diag/tnslsnr/aks02/listener/alert/log.xml
Listening on: (DESCRIPTION=(ADDRESS=(PROTOCOL=tcp)(HOST=95.217.211.31)(PORT=1521)))

Connecting to (DESCRIPTION=(ADDRESS=(PROTOCOL=TCP)(HOST=95.217.211.31)(PORT=1521)))
STATUS of the LISTENER
------------------------
Alias                     listener
Version                   TNSLSNR for Linux: Version 19.0.0.0.0 - Production
Start Date                21-MAY-2024 14:01:33
Uptime                    0 days 0 hr. 0 min. 0 sec
Trace Level               off
Security                  ON: Local OS Authentication
SNMP                      OFF
Listener Parameter File   /u01/app/oracle/product/19.3/db_home/network/admin/listener.ora
Listener Log File         /u01/app/oracle/diag/tnslsnr/aks02/listener/alert/log.xml
Listening Endpoints Summary...
  (DESCRIPTION=(ADDRESS=(PROTOCOL=tcp)(HOST=95.217.211.31)(PORT=1521)))
Services Summary...
Service "CDB_STB_DGMGRL" has 1 instance(s).
  Instance "CDB", status UNKNOWN, has 1 handler(s) for this service...
The command completed successfully
[oracle@aks02 admin]$
```

```
[oracle@aks02 admin]$ exit
logout
[root@aks02 ~]#
[root@aks02 ~]#
[root@aks02 ~]# firewall-cmd --zone=public --add-port=1521/tcp --permanent
success
[root@aks02 ~]#
[root@aks02 ~]#
[root@aks02 ~]# firewall-cmd --reload
success
[root@aks02 ~]#
```

```
[root@aks02 ~]# su - oracle
Last login: Tue May 21 13:56:47 CEST 2024 on pts/1
[oracle@aks02 ~]$
[oracle@aks02 ~]$
[oracle@aks02 ~]$
[oracle@aks02 ~]$ tnsping cdb

TNS Ping Utility for Linux: Version 19.0.0.0.0 - Production on 21-MAY-2024 14:03:57

Copyright (c) 1997, 2019, Oracle.  All rights reserved.

Used parameter files:


Used TNSNAMES adapter to resolve the alias
Attempting to contact (DESCRIPTION = (ADDRESS_LIST = (ADDRESS = (PROTOCOL = TCP)(HOST = 65.109.170.250)(PORT = 1521))) (CO
NNECT_DATA = (SID = CDB)))
OK (0 msec)
[oracle@aks02 ~]$
```

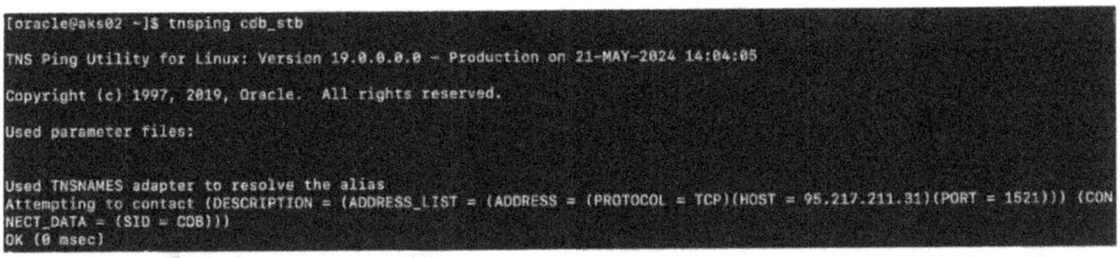
[oracle@aks02 ~]$ tnsping cdb_stb
TNS Ping Utility for Linux: Version 19.0.0.0.0 - Production on 21-MAY-2024 14:04:05
Copyright (c) 1997, 2019, Oracle. All rights reserved.
Used parameter files:
Used TNSNAMES adapter to resolve the alias
Attempting to contact (DESCRIPTION = (ADDRESS_LIST = (ADDRESS = (PROTOCOL = TCP)(HOST = 95.217.211.31)(PORT = 1521))) (CON
NECT_DATA = (SID = CDB)))
OK (0 msec)

Configure redo transport

Note: if you plan to use Oracle Data Guard broker, then you can skip this section “configure redo transport” and jump to “Build Standby” section

Configure redo transport from primary to standby: The below statement says that if the current database is in primary role, then transport logs to standby. We need to change service and db_unique_name for same parameter on standby server

Async: Primary will NOT WAIT until transaction is applied on standby.
Sync: Primary will not WAIT until transaction is applied on standby.

On Primary Server

```
SQL> alter system set log_archive_dest_2 =
'service= CDB_STB async
valid_for=(online_logfiles,primary_role)
db_unique_name=CDB_STB';
```

```
[oracle@aks01 ~]$ sqlplus / as sysdba

SQL*Plus: Release 19.0.0.0.0 - Production on Thu May 23 12:44:19 2024
Version 19.3.0.0.0

Copyright (c) 1982, 2019, Oracle.  All rights reserved.


Connected to:
Oracle Database 19c Enterprise Edition Release 19.0.0.0.0 - Production
Version 19.3.0.0.0

SQL>
```

```
SQL> alter system set log_archive_dest_2 = 'service=CDB_STB async valid_for=(online_logfiles,primary_role) db_unique_name=
CDB_STB';

System altered.
```

```
SQL> show parameter log_archive_dest_2

NAME                                 TYPE        VALUE
------------------------------------ ----------- ------------------------------
log_archive_dest_2                   string      service=cdb_stb async valid_fo
                                                 r=(online_logfiles,primary_rol
                                                 e) db_unique_name=cdb_stb
```

Set FAL_SERVER: Fetch Archive Log parameter tells primary as to where it will get archives from

```
SQL> alter system set fal_server =
'cdb_stb';
```

```
SQL> alter system set fal_server = 'cdb_stb';

System altered.
```

Set dg_config parameter: This parameter defines which databases are in data guard configuration

```
SQL> alter system set log_archive_config =
'dg_config=(CDB, CDB_STB)';
```

```
SQL> alter system set log_archive_config = 'dg_config=(CDB,CDB_STB)';

System altered.

SQL>
```

Build standby

Create pfile on primary, open it and create the necessary directories on the standby server

On Primary Server

```
SQL> create pfile from spfile;
exit
$ cd $ORACLE_HOME/dbs
$ cat initCDB.ora
```

```
SQL> create pfile from spfile;

File created.

SQL>
SQL>
SQL> exit
Disconnected from Oracle Database 19c Enterprise Edition Release 19.0.0.0.0 - Production
Version 19.3.0.0.0
[oracle@aks01 ~]$
[oracle@aks01 ~]$
[oracle@aks01 ~]$ cd $ORACLE_HOME/dbs
```

```
[oracle@aks01 dbs]$ cat initCDB.ora
CDB.__data_transfer_cache_size=0
CDB.__db_cache_size=1090519040
CDB.__inmemory_ext_roarea=0
CDB.__inmemory_ext_rwarea=0
CDB.__java_pool_size=0
CDB.__large_pool_size=16777216
CDB.__oracle_base='/u01/app/oracle'#ORACLE_BASE set from environment
CDB.__pga_aggregate_target=536870912
CDB.__sga_target=1577058304
CDB.__shared_io_pool_size=83886080
CDB.__shared_pool_size=369098752
CDB.__streams_pool_size=0
CDB.__unified_pga_pool_size=0
*.audit_file_dest='/u01/app/oracle/admin/CDB/adump'
*.audit_trail='db'
*.compatible='19.0.0'
*.control_files='/u01/CDB/control01.ctl','/u01/CDB/control02.ctl'
*.db_block_size=8192
*.db_name='CDB'
*.db_recovery_file_dest_size=21474836480
*.db_recovery_file_dest='/u01/CDB/FRA'
*.diagnostic_dest='/u01/app/oracle'
```

On Standby Server

Create directories as you find in the initCDB.ora file

```
mkdir -p /u01/app/oracle/admin/CDB/adump
/u01/CDB/ /u01/CDB/FRA/ /u01/app/oracle
```

```
[oracle@aks02 ~]$ env|grep ROA
[oracle@aks02 ~]$ env|grep ORA
ORACLE_SID=CDB
ORACLE_BASE=/u01/app/oracle
ORACLE_HOME=/u01/app/oracle/product/19.3/db_home
[oracle@aks02 ~]$
```

```
[oracle@aks02 ~]$ mkdir -p /u01/app/oracle/admin/CDB/adump /u01/CDB/ /u01/CDB/FRA /u01/app/oracle
[oracle@aks02 ~]$
```

On standby server, create parameter file with just db_name parameter and start the instance in nomount mode

On Standby Server

```
cd $ORACLE_HOME/dbs
vi initCDB.ora


*.db_name='CDB' ---> Save it

$ env|grep ORA
$ sqlplus / as sysdba

SQL> STARTUP NOMOUNT;
SQL> exit;

--you must exit from sqlplus, else cloning
will fail
```

```
[oracle@aks02 ~]$ cd $ORACLE_HOME/dbs
[oracle@aks02 dbs]$
[oracle@aks02 dbs]$
[oracle@aks02 dbs]$
[oracle@aks02 dbs]$ vi initCDB.ora
```

```
*.db_name='CDB'
~
```

```
[oracle@aks02 dbs]$ env|grep ORA
ORACLE_SID=CDB
ORACLE_BASE=/u01/app/oracle
ORACLE_HOME=/u01/app/oracle/product/19.3/db_home
[oracle@aks02 dbs]$
```

```
[oracle@aks02 dbs]$ sqlplus / as sysdba

SQL*Plus: Release 19.0.0.0.0 - Production on Thu May 23 13:04:28 2024
Version 19.3.0.0.0

Copyright (c) 1982, 2019, Oracle.  All rights reserved.

Connected to an idle instance.

SQL> startup nomount;
ORACLE instance started.

Total System Global Area  285211696 bytes
Fixed Size                  8895536 bytes
Variable Size             218103808 bytes
Database Buffers           50331648 bytes
Redo Buffers                7880704 bytes
SQL>
```

```
[oracle@aks02 dbs]$ ps -ef|grep pmon
oracle   25256     1  0 13:04 ?        00:00:00 ora_pmon_CDB
oracle   25342 24131  0 13:04 pts/0    00:00:00 grep --color=auto pmon
[oracle@aks02 dbs]$
```

On Primary Server

```
[oracle@aks01 dbs]$ cd
[oracle@aks01 ~]$
[oracle@aks01 ~]$
[oracle@aks01 ~]$
[oracle@aks01 ~]$ ssh-keygen
Generating public/private rsa key pair.
Enter file in which to save the key (/home/oracle/.ssh/id_rsa):
Enter passphrase (empty for no passphrase):
Enter same passphrase again:
Your identification has been saved in /home/oracle/.ssh/id_rsa.
Your public key has been saved in /home/oracle/.ssh/id_rsa.pub.
The key fingerprint is:
SHA256:bWe2T+Lq266wCy0XB36QUfa6UW4fIjNNPTG5aF/olkc oracle@aks01.dbageneis.com
The key's randomart image is:
+---[RSA 2048]----+
|         ..o   o. |
|          + . ..o |
|         +   +.oo |
|        . + *o o.E|
|         S @.Oo.+ |
|        . = @ +=..|
|       o + . o.o. |
|        + o o +   |
|         oo==+ .  |
+----[SHA256]-----+
[oracle@aks01 ~]$
```

```
[oracle@aks01 ~]$ ls -lart
total 36
-rw-r--r--  1 oracle oinstall  231 Nov 24  2021 .bashrc
-rw-r--r--  1 oracle oinstall   18 Nov 24  2021 .bash_logout
-rw-r--r--  1 oracle oinstall  172 Aug  9  2022 .kshrc
drwxr-xr-x. 3 root   root     4096 May 21 12:49 ..
-rw-r--r--  1 oracle oinstall  314 May 21 12:52 .bash_profile
drwxr-x---  2 oracle oinstall 4096 May 21 13:04 .oracle_jre_usage
drwx------  4 oracle oinstall 4096 May 21 13:04 .
-rw-------  1 oracle oinstall 2439 May 22 15:44 .bash_history
drwx------  2 oracle oinstall 4096 May 23 13:07 .ssh
[oracle@aks01 ~]$
```

```
[oracle@aks01 ~]$ cd .ssh
[oracle@aks01 .ssh]$
[oracle@aks01 .ssh]$
[oracle@aks01 .ssh]$ ls -lrt
total 12
-rw-r--r-- 1 oracle oinstall  175 May 23 13:06 known_hosts
-rw-r--r-- 1 oracle oinstall  408 May 23 13:07 id_rsa.pub
-rw------- 1 oracle oinstall 1679 May 23 13:07 id_rsa
[oracle@aks01 .ssh]$
```

Get the public key

```
cat id_rsa.pub
```

```
[oracle@aks01 .ssh]$
[oracle@aks01 .ssh]$ cat id_rsa.pub
ssh-rsa AAAAB3NzaC1yc2EAAAADAQABAAABAQDUuKgrWfsHtdlKWIFibTz3uklpt12YQTwNRle7uMjS0De5dyqwJh2zUmm+IqvAWKrV+qitkBae+BN+r0Yar/
8BGDzBk+ID5jya1xFjGrGsMWrPtIKU6kR/2Ay0o2OmC3g8NwiSYcNuAbzcFoE1Ui30EVSoQa6wHKR2B39GQ30Yuv5GCJF07ybv4bOxLmcAr8CpFvUFw843Ps14
RnjeHpUIFlye3uAn/MPX0mKrpw9Da8wlXmtZGmNIWuCbJFxjGp9vUh3ryCpeuvYLlx/reihAN3QqRXv+UL8hiCbdVHT1d27ER/cN5XI97pHDH9ZLS0CaeXyTv3
WHtZOxLK8jt+6N oracle@aks01.dbageneis.com
[oracle@aks01 .ssh]$
```

On Standby Server

```
[oracle@aks02 dbs]$ ps -ef|grep pmon
oracle   25256     1  0 13:04 ?        00:00:00 ora_pmon_CDB
oracle   25342 24131  0 13:04 pts/0    00:00:00 grep --color=auto pmon
[oracle@aks02 dbs]$
[oracle@aks02 dbs]$
[oracle@aks02 dbs]$
[oracle@aks02 dbs]$ cd
[oracle@aks02 ~]$
[oracle@aks02 ~]$
[oracle@aks02 ~]$
[oracle@aks02 ~]$ ls -lart
total 32
-rw-r--r--  1 oracle oinstall  231 Nov 24  2021 .bashrc
-rw-r--r--  1 oracle oinstall   18 Nov 24  2021 .bash_logout
-rw-r--r--  1 oracle oinstall  172 Aug  9  2022 .kshrc
drwxr-xr-x. 3 root   root     4096 May 21 12:50 ..
-rw-r--r--  1 oracle oinstall  314 May 21 12:52 .bash_profile
drwx------  2 oracle oinstall 4096 May 21 12:57 .ssh
drwx------  3 oracle oinstall 4096 May 21 12:57 .
-rw-------  1 oracle oinstall 1428 May 21 16:24 .bash_history
[oracle@aks02 ~]$
```

```
[oracle@aks02 ~]$ cd .ssh
[oracle@aks02 .ssh]$
[oracle@aks02 .ssh]$
[oracle@aks02 .ssh]$
[oracle@aks02 .ssh]$ ls
[oracle@aks02 .ssh]$
[oracle@aks02 .ssh]$ vi authorized_keys
```

Copy the public key from the primary server and past it

```
ssh-rsa AAAAB3NzaC1yc2EAAAADAQABAAABAQDUuKgrWfsHtdlKWIFibTz3uklpt12YQTwNRle7uMjS0De5dyqwJh2zUmm+IqvAWKrV+qitkBae+BN+r0Yar/
8BGDzBk+ID5jya1xFjGrGsMWrPtIKU6kR/2Ay0o2OmC3g8NwiSYcNuAbzcFoE1Ui30EVSoQa6wHKR2B39GQ30Yuv5GCJF07ybv4bOxLmcAr8CpFvUFw843Ps14
RnjeHpUIFlye3uAn/MPX0mKrpw9Da8wlXmtZGmNIWuCbJFxjGp9vUh3ryCpeuvYLlx/reihAN3QqRXv+UL8hiCbdVHT1d27ER/cN5XI97pHDH9ZLS0CaeXyTv3
WHtZOxLK8jt+6N oracle@aks01.dbageneis.com
```

```
[oracle@aks02 .ssh]$ chmod 600 authorized_keys
[oracle@aks02 .ssh]$
```

Now our passwordless connection is set up between the primary and standby.

On Primary Server

```
[oracle@aks01 .ssh]$ cd $ORACLE_HOME/dbs
[oracle@aks01 dbs]$
[oracle@aks01 dbs]$
[oracle@aks01 dbs]$ ls -lrt
total 18312
-rw-r--r-- 1 oracle oinstall     3079 May 14  2015 init.ora
-rw-r----- 1 oracle oinstall       24 May 21 13:02 lkCDB
-rw-r----- 1 oracle oinstall     2048 May 21 13:04 orapwCDB
-rw-rw---- 1 oracle oinstall     1544 May 21 13:26 hc_CDB.dat
-rw-r----- 1 oracle oinstall 18726912 May 21 13:55 snapcf_CDB.f
-rw-r----- 1 oracle oinstall     3584 May 23 12:59 spfileCDB.ora
-rw-r--r-- 1 oracle oinstall     1240 May 23 13:00 initCDB.ora
[oracle@aks01 dbs]$
[oracle@aks01 dbs]$
[oracle@aks01 dbs]$ scp orapwCDB oracle@95.217.211.31:$ORACLE_HOME/dbs
orapwCDB                                              100% 2048     2.6MB/s   00:00
[oracle@aks01 dbs]$
```

On Standby Server

```
[oracle@aks02 .ssh]$ cd $ORACLE_HOME/dbs
[oracle@aks02 dbs]$
[oracle@aks02 dbs]$
[oracle@aks02 dbs]$ ls -lrt
total 16
-rw-r--r-- 1 oracle oinstall 3079 May 14  2015 init.ora
-rw-r--r-- 1 oracle oinstall   16 May 23 13:04 initCDB.ora
-rw-rw---- 1 oracle oinstall 1544 May 23 13:04 hc_CDB.dat
-rw-r----- 1 oracle oinstall 2048 May 23 13:11 orapwCDB
[oracle@aks02 dbs]$
```

Duplicate primary database via RMAN: On primary, connect to RMAN, specifying a full connect string for both the TARGET and AUXILIARY instances. Do not attempt to use OS authentication else, the cloning will fail

To DORECOVERY option starts recovery by applying all available logs immediately after restore

On Primary Server

```
rman target sys@cdb auxiliary sys@cdb_stb
```

```
[oracle@aks01 dbs]$ rman target sys@cdb auxiliary sys@cdb_stb

Recovery Manager: Release 19.0.0.0.0 - Production on Thu May 23 13:14:02 2024
Version 19.3.0.0.0

Copyright (c) 1982, 2019, Oracle and/or its affiliates.  All rights reserved.

target database Password:
connected to target database: CDB (DBID=2286160971)
auxiliary database Password:
connected to auxiliary database: CDB (not mounted)

RMAN>
```

```
RMAN> DUPLICATE TARGET DATABASE FOR STANDBY
FROM ACTIVE DATABASE DORECOVER
SPFILE
SET db_unique_name='CDB_STB'
SET fal_server='CDB'
SET log_archive_dest_2='service=CDB async
valid_for=(online_logfiles,primary_role)
db_unique_name=CDB'
NOFILENAMECHECK;
```

```
RMAN> DUPLICATE TARGET DATABASE FOR STANDBY
FROM ACTIVE DATABASE DORECOVER
SPFILE
SET db_unique_name='CDB_STB'
SET fal_server='CDB'
SET log_archive_dest_2='service=CDB async valid_for=(online_logfiles,primary_role) db_unique_name=CDB'
NOFILENAMECHECK;2> 3> 4> 5> 6> 7>

Starting Duplicate Db at 23-MAY-24
using target database control file instead of recovery catalog
allocated channel: ORA_AUX_DISK_1
```

Once cloning is done, you should see below at RMAN prompt

```
Finished Duplicate Db at 23-MAY-24
```

Enable flashback on standby: As we know the importance of flashback in data guard, we must enable it on standby as well

On Standby Server

```
SQL> alter database flashback on;
```

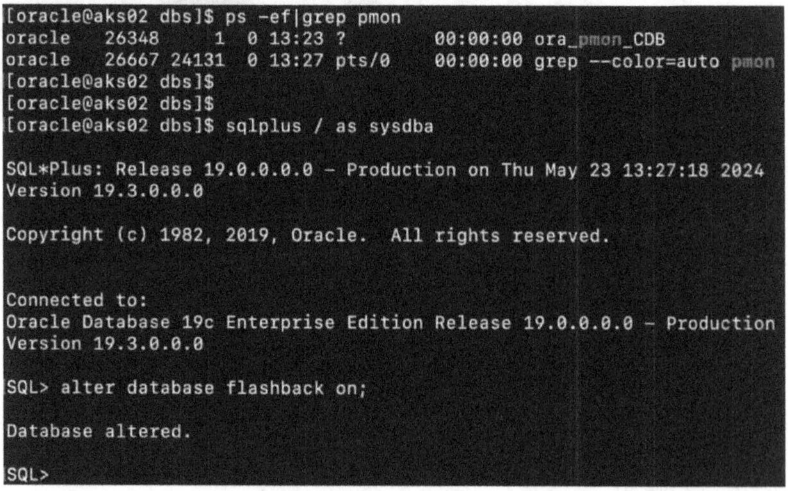

```
[oracle@aks02 dbs]$ ps -ef|grep pmon
oracle   26348     1  0 13:23 ?        00:00:00 ora_pmon_CDB
oracle   26667 24131  0 13:27 pts/0    00:00:00 grep --color=auto pmon
[oracle@aks02 dbs]$
[oracle@aks02 dbs]$
[oracle@aks02 dbs]$ sqlplus / as sysdba

SQL*Plus: Release 19.0.0.0.0 - Production on Thu May 23 13:27:18 2024
Version 19.3.0.0.0

Copyright (c) 1982, 2019, Oracle.  All rights reserved.


Connected to:
Oracle Database 19c Enterprise Edition Release 19.0.0.0.0 - Production
Version 19.3.0.0.0

SQL> alter database flashback on;

Database altered.

SQL>
```

Bounce database & start MRP (Apply Service): It's good to bounce standby, put it in mount mode and start MRP process

On Standby Server

```
SQL> shut immediate;
SQL> startup mount;
```

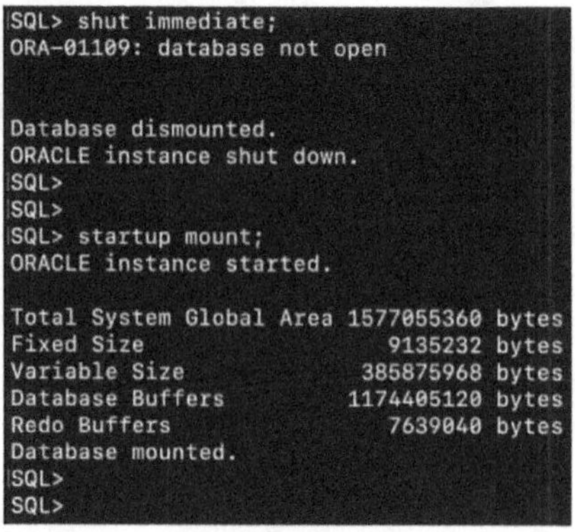

```
SQL> shut immediate;
ORA-01109: database not open


Database dismounted.
ORACLE instance shut down.
SQL>
SQL>
SQL> startup mount;
ORACLE instance started.

Total System Global Area 1577055360 bytes
Fixed Size                  9135232 bytes
Variable Size             385875968 bytes
Database Buffers         1174405120 bytes
Redo Buffers                7639040 bytes
Database mounted.
SQL>
SQL>
```

```
SQL> select name, open_mode, db_unique_name, database_role from v$database;

NAME      OPEN_MODE            DB_UNIQUE_NAME                 DATABASE_ROLE
--------- -------------------- ------------------------------ ----------------
CDB       MOUNTED              CDB_STB                        PHYSICAL STANDBY

SQL>
```

On Primary Server

```
RMAN> exit


Recovery Manager complete.
[oracle@aks01 dbs]$
[oracle@aks01 dbs]$
[oracle@aks01 dbs]$ sqlplus / as sysdba

SQL*Plus: Release 19.0.0.0.0 - Production on Thu May 23 13:30:28 2024
Version 19.3.0.0.0

Copyright (c) 1982, 2019, Oracle.  All rights reserved.


Connected to:
Oracle Database 19c Enterprise Edition Release 19.0.0.0.0 - Production
Version 19.3.0.0.0

SQL>
```

Let us start the apply service on the standby server

```
SQL> alter database recover managed standby
database disconnect;
```

```
SQL> alter database recover managed standby database disconnect;

Database altered.

SQL>
```

Verify standby configuration

Once MRP is started, we must verify which archive log number MRP is applying on standby

On Standby Server

```
select process, status, sequence# from
v$managed_standby;
```

```
SQL> select process, status, sequence# from v$managed_standby;

PROCESS   STATUS        SEQUENCE#
--------- ------------ ----------
ARCH      CONNECTED             0
DGRD      ALLOCATED             0
DGRD      ALLOCATED             0
ARCH      CONNECTED             0
ARCH      CONNECTED             0
ARCH      CONNECTED             0
RFS       IDLE                  0
RFS       IDLE                 13
MRP0      APPLYING_LOG         13

9 rows selected.

SQL>
```

On Primary Server

```
SQL> archive log list;
Database log mode              Archive Mode
Automatic archival             Enabled
Archive destination            USE_DB_RECOVERY_FILE_DEST
Oldest online log sequence     11
Next log sequence to archive   13
Current log sequence           13
SQL>
```

```
SQL> alter system switch logfile;

System altered.

SQL> /

System altered.

SQL> /
/

System altered.

SQL>
System altered.

SQL>
```

On Standby Server

```
SQL> /

PROCESS   STATUS       SEQUENCE#
--------- ------------ ----------
ARCH      CLOSING              14
DGRD      ALLOCATED             0
DGRD      ALLOCATED             0
ARCH      CONNECTED             0
ARCH      CLOSING              16
ARCH      CLOSING              15
RFS       IDLE                  0
RFS       IDLE                 17
MRP0      APPLYING_LOG         17
RFS       IDLE                  0

10 rows selected.
```

```
SQL> /

PROCESS   STATUS       SEQUENCE#
--------- ------------ ----------
ARCH      CLOSING              14
DGRD      ALLOCATED             0
DGRD      ALLOCATED             0
ARCH      CONNECTED             0
ARCH      CLOSING              16
ARCH      CLOSING              15
RFS       IDLE                  0
RFS       IDLE                 17
MRP0      APPLYING_LOG         17
RFS       IDLE                  0

10 rows selected.

SQL>
```

On Primary Server

Let us check whether everything is fine or not.

```
SQL> archive log list;
Database log mode              Archive Mode
Automatic archival             Enabled
Archive destination            USE_DB_RECOVERY_FILE_DEST
Oldest online log sequence     15
Next log sequence to archive   17
Current log sequence           17
SQL>
SQL>
```

On Standby Server

```
SQL> select process, status, sequence# from v$managed_standby;

PROCESS   STATUS       SEQUENCE#
--------- ------------ ----------
ARCH      CLOSING              14
DGRD      ALLOCATED             0
DGRD      ALLOCATED             0
ARCH      CONNECTED             0
ARCH      CLOSING              16
ARCH      CLOSING              15
RFS       IDLE                  0
RFS       IDLE                 17
MRP0      APPLYING_LOG         17
RFS       IDLE                  0

10 rows selected.

SQL>
```

The MRP0 APPLYING_LOG number should match from the current log sequence on the primary server.

On Primary Server

```
SQL> alter system switch logfile;

System altered.

SQL>
SQL> archive log list;
Database log mode              Archive Mode
Automatic archival             Enabled
Archive destination            USE_DB_RECOVERY_FILE_DEST
Oldest online log sequence     16
Next log sequence to archive   18
Current log sequence           18
SQL>
```

On Standby Server

```
SQL> select process, status, sequence# from v$managed_standby;

PROCESS   STATUS       SEQUENCE#
--------- ------------ ----------
ARCH      CLOSING              14
DGRD      ALLOCATED             0
DGRD      ALLOCATED             0
ARCH      CLOSING              17
ARCH      CLOSING              16
ARCH      CLOSING              15
RFS       IDLE                  0
RFS       IDLE                 18
MRP0      APPLYING_LOG         18
RFS       IDLE                  0

10 rows selected.

SQL>
```

How do we stop the apply service?

On Primary Server

```
SQL> ALTER DATABASE RECOVER MANAGED STANDBY DATABASE CANCEL;

Database altered.

SQL>
SQL>
SQL> select process, status, sequence# from v$managed_standby;

PROCESS   STATUS       SEQUENCE#
--------- ------------ ----------
ARCH      CLOSING              14
DGRD      ALLOCATED             0
DGRD      ALLOCATED             0
ARCH      CLOSING              17
ARCH      CLOSING              16
ARCH      CLOSING              15
RFS       IDLE                  0
RFS       IDLE                 18
RFS       IDLE                  0

9 rows selected.

SQL>
```

If we stop the apply service, does that mean any archives that are generated from primary, they will not come to SRLs or they will come and reside on SRLs?

LNS is active so any logs that are generated on primary, they will still be sent to standby and they will be residing under SRLs. When we start the apply service, it will start applying the archives as and when it finds them available.

Example: Let us perform some log switches on primary

```
SQL> alter system switch logfile;

System altered.

SQL>
SQL> /
/

System altered.

SQL>
System altered.

SQL> /

System altered.

SQL> /
/
/

System altered.
```

```
SQL> archive log list;
Database log mode              Archive Mode
Automatic archival             Enabled
Archive destination            USE_DB_RECOVERY_FILE_DEST
Oldest online log sequence     24
Next log sequence to archive   26
Current log sequence           26
SQL>
```

On Standby Server

```
SQL> select process, status, sequence# from v$managed_standby;

PROCESS   STATUS        SEQUENCE#
--------- ------------ ----------
ARCH      CLOSING              25
DGRD      ALLOCATED             0
DGRD      ALLOCATED             0
ARCH      CLOSING              23
ARCH      CLOSING              22
ARCH      CLOSING              24
RFS       IDLE                  0
RFS       IDLE                 26
RFS       IDLE                  0
RFS       IDLE                  0

10 rows selected.
```

Let us start the MRP / Apply process

```
SQL> alter database recover managed standby database disconnect;

Database altered.

SQL> select process, status, sequence# from v$managed_standby;

PROCESS   STATUS        SEQUENCE#
--------- ------------ ----------
ARCH      CLOSING              25
DGRD      ALLOCATED             0
DGRD      ALLOCATED             0
ARCH      CLOSING              23
ARCH      CLOSING              22
ARCH      CLOSING              24
RFS       IDLE                  0
RFS       IDLE                 26
RFS       IDLE                  0
RFS       IDLE                  0
MRP0      APPLYING_LOG         26

11 rows selected.

SQL>
```

How do we start and stop the LNS services?

```
SQL> show parameter dest_2;

NAME                                 TYPE        VALUE
------------------------------------ ----------- ------------------------------
db_create_online_log_dest_2          string
log_archive_dest_2                   string      service=CDB_STB async valid_fo
                                                 r=(online_logfiles,primary_rol
                                                 e) db_unique_name=CDB_STB
log_archive_dest_20                  string
log_archive_dest_21                  string
log_archive_dest_22                  string
log_archive_dest_23                  string
log_archive_dest_24                  string
log_archive_dest_25                  string
log_archive_dest_26                  string

NAME                                 TYPE        VALUE
------------------------------------ ----------- ------------------------------
log_archive_dest_27                  string
log_archive_dest_28                  string
log_archive_dest_29                  string
SQL>
```

```
SQL> alter system set log_archive_dest_state_2='DEFER';

System altered.

SQL>
SQL> show parameter dest_2;

NAME                                 TYPE        VALUE
------------------------------------ ----------- ------------------------------
db_create_online_log_dest_2          string
log_archive_dest_2                   string      service=CDB_STB async valid_fo
                                                 r=(online_logfiles,primary_rol
                                                 e) db_unique_name=CDB_STB
log_archive_dest_20                  string
log_archive_dest_21                  string
log_archive_dest_22                  string
log_archive_dest_23                  string
log_archive_dest_24                  string
log_archive_dest_25                  string
log_archive_dest_26                  string

NAME                                 TYPE        VALUE
------------------------------------ ----------- ------------------------------
log_archive_dest_27                  string
log_archive_dest_28                  string
log_archive_dest_29                  string
SQL>
```

```
SQL> archive log list;
Database log mode              Archive Mode
Automatic archival             Enabled
Archive destination            USE_DB_RECOVERY_FILE_DEST
Oldest online log sequence     24
Next log sequence to archive   26
Current log sequence           26
SQL>
SQL>
SQL>
SQL> alter system switch logfile;

System altered.

SQL> /

System altered.

SQL> /

System altered.

SQL> /

System altered.
```

On Standby Server

```
SQL> select process, status, sequence# from v$managed_standby;

PROCESS   STATUS       SEQUENCE#
--------- ------------ ----------
ARCH      CLOSING              25
DGRD      ALLOCATED             0
DGRD      ALLOCATED             0
ARCH      CLOSING              26
ARCH      CLOSING              22
ARCH      CLOSING              24
RFS       IDLE                  0
RFS       IDLE                  0
MRP0      WAIT_FOR_LOG         27

9 rows selected.
```

How do we cleanly shutdown the standby?

On Standby Server

```
alter database recover managed standby
database cancel;
shut immediate;
```

```
SQL> alter database recover managed standby database cancel;

Database altered.

SQL>
SQL>
SQL> shut immediate;
ORA-01109: database not open


Database dismounted.
ORACLE instance shut down.
```

How do we start the standby and bring it in sync?

On Standby Server

```
SQL> exit
Disconnected from Oracle Database 19c Enterprise Edition Release 19.0.0.0.0 - Production
Version 19.3.0.0.0
```

```
[oracle@aks02 ~]$ sqlplus / as sysdba

SQL*Plus: Release 19.0.0.0.0 - Production on Fri May 24 13:27:38 2024
Version 19.3.0.0.0

Copyright (c) 1982, 2019, Oracle.  All rights reserved.

Connected to an idle instance.

SQL> startup mount;
ORACLE instance started.

Total System Global Area 1577055360 bytes
Fixed Size                  9135232 bytes
Variable Size             385875968 bytes
Database Buffers         1174405120 bytes
Redo Buffers                7639040 bytes
Database mounted.
SQL>
```

```
SQL> alter database recover managed standby database disconnect;

Database altered.

SQL>
SQL>
SQL> select process, status, sequence# from v$managed_standby;

PROCESS   STATUS       SEQUENCE#
--------- ------------ ----------
ARCH      CONNECTED             0
DGRD      ALLOCATED             0
DGRD      ALLOCATED             0
ARCH      CONNECTED             0
ARCH      CONNECTED             0
ARCH      CONNECTED             0
RFS       IDLE                 33
RFS       IDLE                  0
MRP0      APPLYING_LOG         33

9 rows selected.

SQL>
```

On Primary Server

```
SQL> archive log list;
Database log mode              Archive Mode
Automatic archival             Enabled
Archive destination            USE_DB_RECOVERY_FILE_DEST
Oldest online log sequence     31
Next log sequence to archive   33
Current log sequence           33
SQL>
```

CHAPTER 3

Data Guard Client Connectivity

Anything we create on the primary will automatically be created on the standby. Let's create a service on the primary, and since the logs are switched, that service will automatically be created on the standby. However, this service will have a special rule: it will be enabled only when the database role is primary. This means that when we perform a switchover and the roles change—primary becomes standby and standby becomes primary—the service will go down on the former primary and come up on the new primary.

Services in Oracle

Listener will listen for database or service. Listener parameter will accept the connection for SID / Services.

Example: listener.ora file

The below is the default listener configuration

```
LISTENER =
  (DESCRIPTION_LIST =
    (DESCRIPTION =
      (ADDRESS = (PROTOCOL = TCP)(HOST = 192.168.1.7)(PORT = 1521))
    )
  )

SID_LIST_LISTENER =
  (SID_LIST =
    (SID_DESC =
      (ORACLE_HOME = /u01/app/oracle/product/11.2.0.4/db_1)
      (SID_NAME = orcl)
    )
  )
```

In the above example, we can see the SID_NAME = orcl. Basically, we can directly connect to a database using SID_NAME or we can create our own service name. That service name can be different from our database name so that no one will get to know what database we are connecting to.

On Primary Server

```
[oracle@aks01 ~]$ lsnrctl services

LSNRCTL for Linux: Version 19.0.0.0.0 - Production on 24-MAY-2024 13:35:21

Copyright (c) 1991, 2019, Oracle.  All rights reserved.

Connecting to (DESCRIPTION=(ADDRESS=(PROTOCOL=TCP)(HOST=65.109.170.250)(PORT=1521)))
Services Summary...
Service "CDB_DGMGRL" has 1 instance(s).
  Instance "CDB", status UNKNOWN, has 1 handler(s) for this service...
    Handler(s):
      "DEDICATED" established:42 refused:0
         LOCAL SERVER
The command completed successfully
[oracle@aks01 ~]$
```

```
[oracle@aks01 ~]$ sqlplus / as sysdba

SQL*Plus: Release 19.0.0.0.0 - Production on Fri May 24 13:35:44 2024
Version 19.3.0.0.0

Copyright (c) 1982, 2019, Oracle.  All rights reserved.


Connected to:
Oracle Database 19c Enterprise Edition Release 19.0.0.0.0 - Production
Version 19.3.0.0.0
```

```
SQL> show parameter service;

NAME                                 TYPE        VALUE
------------------------------------ ----------- ------
service_names                        string      CDB
SQL>
```

Our listener listens for the service name, which happens to be the same as the database SID. This means every database has a SID, and the service name is the same as the database SID. The listener will listen to that specific SID or service name. However, Oracle also allows us to create our own custom services.

```
Listener => SERVICE (TESTDB)



SID          : E6P
DB NAME      : E6P
SERVICE      : E6P,TESTDB
```

In the above listener configuration, our listener will start accepting connections for the TESTDB service. Anyone connecting to the TESTDB service on the listener will have their connection automatically forwarded to the E6P database. Listeners listen for services, and by default, the service name is the same as the database SID, so it appears that the listener is accepting connections for that specific database. However, we can have more than one service. We can define our own service, and configure the listener to listen only to that particular service.

Client connectivity in Data Guard Configuration:
https://support.dbagenesis.com/post/client-connectivity-in-data-guard-configuration#viewer-dna85

When you have a physical standby, you must make sure client connectivity is set properly so that when you perform a failover or switchover, the client must smoothly connect to the new primary in data guard configuration.

Create New Service on Primary

Let us create the service.

On Primary Server

```
exec DBMS_SERVICE.CREATE_SERVICE
(service_name => 'CDB_HA', network_name =>
CDB_HA', failover_method => 'BASIC',
failover_type => 'SELECT', failover_retries
=> 30, failover_delay => 10);

alter system switch logfile;
```

```
SQL> exec DBMS_SERVICE.CREATE_SERVICE (service_name => 'CDB_HA', network_name => 'CDB_HA', failover_method => 'BASIC', fai
lover_type => 'SELECT', failover_retries => 30, failover_delay => 10);

PL/SQL procedure successfully completed.

SQL>
SQL>
SQL> alter system switch logfile;

System altered.

SQL>
```

Make above service run only on primary: This service should run only on the primary database. Even when there is switchover or failover, this service should continue to run on new primary

On Primary Server

```
select DATABASE_ROLE into v_role from
V$DATABASE;
```

```
SQL> select database_role from v$database;

DATABASE_ROLE
----------------
PRIMARY

SQL>
```

On Standby Server

```
SQL> select database_role from v$database;

DATABASE_ROLE
----------------
PHYSICAL STANDBY

SQL>
```

If the role is primary, the CDB_HA service will start. If the role is not primary, the service will stop.

On Primary Server

```
create or replace procedure start_ha_service
is
v_role VARCHAR(30);
begin
select DATABASE_ROLE into v_role from
V$DATABASE;
if v_role = 'PRIMARY' then
DBMS_SERVICE.START_SERVICE('CDB_HA');
else
DBMS_SERVICE.STOP_SERVICE('CDB_HA');
end if;
end;
/
```

```
SQL> create or replace procedure start_ha_service
is
v_role VARCHAR(30);
begin
select DATABASE_ROLE into v_role from V$DATABASE;
if v_role = 'PRIMARY' then
DBMS_SERVICE.START_SERVICE('CDB_HA');
else
DBMS_SERVICE.STOP_SERVICE('CDB_HA');
end if;
end;
/  2    3    4    5    6    7    8    9   10   11   12

Procedure created.

SQL>
```

Create Trigger to Auto Start Service

We need to create a trigger to start the service on database startup and during role changes on the primary.

On Primary Server

```
TRIGGER TO START SERVICE ON DB STARTUP:
=======================================
create or replace TRIGGER ha_on_startup
after startup on database
begin
start_ha_service;
end;
/
```

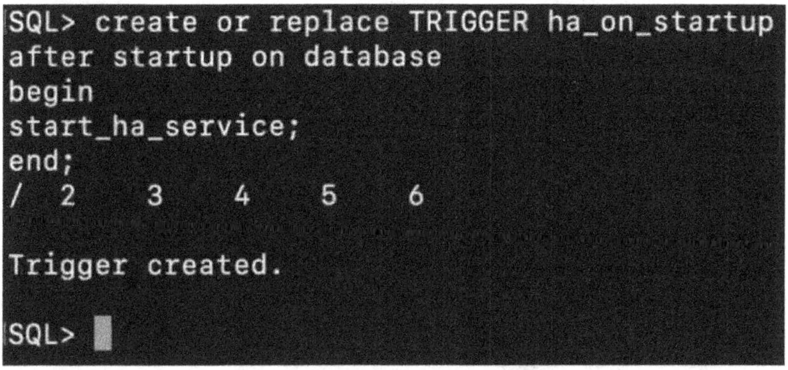
SQL> create or replace TRIGGER ha_on_startup
after startup on database
begin
start_ha_service;
end;
/ 2 3 4 5 6
Trigger created.
SQL>

```
TRIGGER TO START SERVICE ON DB ROLECHANGE:
==========================================
create or replace TRIGGER ha_on_role_change
after db_role_change on database
begin
start_ha_service;
end;
/
```

```
SQL> create or replace TRIGGER ha_on_role_change
after db_role_change on database
begin
start_ha_service;
end;
/  2    3    4    5    6

Trigger created.

SQL>
```

Start the new service on primary

```
SQL> exec start_ha_service;
SQL> alter system archive log current;
```

```
SQL> exec start_ha_service;

PL/SQL procedure successfully completed.

SQL>
```

```
SQL> desc v$active_services;
 Name                                      Null?    Type
 ----------------------------------------- -------- ----------------
 SERVICE_ID                                         NUMBER
 NAME                                               VARCHAR2(64)
 NAME_HASH                                          NUMBER
 NETWORK_NAME                                       VARCHAR2(512)
 CREATION_DATE                                      DATE
 CREATION_DATE_HASH                                 NUMBER
 GOAL                                               VARCHAR2(12)
 DTP                                                VARCHAR2(1)
 BLOCKED                                            CHAR(2)
 AQ_HA_NOTIFICATION                                 VARCHAR2(3)
 CLB_GOAL                                           VARCHAR2(5)
 COMMIT_OUTCOME                                     VARCHAR2(3)
 RETENTION_TIME                                     NUMBER
 REPLAY_INITIATION_TIMEOUT                          NUMBER
 SESSION_STATE_CONSISTENCY                          VARCHAR2(128)
 GLOBAL                                             VARCHAR2(3)
 CON_NAME                                           VARCHAR2(128)
 SQL_TRANSLATION_PROFILE                            VARCHAR2(261)
 MAX_LAG_TIME                                       VARCHAR2(128)
 STOP_OPTION                                        VARCHAR2(128)
```

```
SQL> select name, network_name from v$active_services;
```

```
----------------
NETWORK_NAME
----------------
CDB_HA
CDB_HA

pdb2
pdb2

SYS$BACKGROUND
```

```
SQL> alter system switch logfile;

System altered.

SQL>
```

```
SQL> exit
Disconnected from Oracle Database 19c Enterprise Edition Release 19.0.0.0.0 - Productio
Version 19.3.0.0.0
[oracle@aks01 ~]$
```

Listener Errors

```
Listener error:
    - check /etc/hosts
    - bounce listener
    - alter system register;
```

Enable Client Connect in Data Guard

Update client's tns entries to access Oracle Data Guard setup via above service

```
CDB_ARUN =
   (DESCRIPTION =
     (ADDRESS_LIST=
       (ADDRESS = (PROTOCOL = TCP)(HOST =
aks01.ddbagenesis.com)(PORT = 1521))
       (ADDRESS = (PROTOCOL = TCP)(HOST =
aks02.ddbagenesis.com)(PORT = 1521))
     )
    (CONNECT_DATA = (SERVICE_NAME = CDB_HR)

(FAILOVER_MODE=(TYPE=SELECT)(METHOD=BASIC)(R
ETRIES=30)(DELAY=10))
    )
   )

vi $ORACLE_HOME/network/admin/tnsnames.ora

tnsping CDB_ARUN

Sql sys/enterCDB#123@cdb_arun as sysdba
```

On Primary Server

```
[oracle@aks01 ~]$ cd $ORACLE_HOME/network/admin
[oracle@aks01 admin]$
[oracle@aks01 admin]$
[oracle@aks01 admin]$ ls
listener.ora  samples  shrept.lst  tnsnames.ora
[oracle@aks01 admin]$
[oracle@aks01 admin]$
[oracle@aks01 admin]$ cat listener.ora
LISTENER =
  (DESCRIPTION_LIST =
    (DESCRIPTION =
      (ADDRESS = (PROTOCOL = TCP)(HOST = aks01.dbagenesis.com)(PORT = 1521))
      (ADDRESS = (PROTOCOL = IPC)(KEY = EXTPROC1521))
    )
  )

SID_LIST_LISTENER =
  (SID_LIST =
    (SID_DESC =
      (GLOBAL_DBNAME = CDB_DGMGRL)
      (ORACLE_HOME = /u01/app/oracle/product/19.3/db_home)
      (SID_NAME = CDB)
    )
  )

ADR_BASE_LISTENER = /u01/app/oracle
[oracle@aks01 admin]$
```

On Standby Server

```
[oracle@aks02 admin]$ ls -lrt
total 16
-rw-r--r-- 1 oracle oinstall 1536 Feb 14  2018 shrept.lst
drwxr-xr-x 2 oracle oinstall 4096 Apr 17  2019 samples
-rw-r--r-- 1 oracle oinstall  340 May 21 13:57 tnsnames.ora
-rw-r--r-- 1 oracle oinstall  358 May 25 08:36 listener.ora
[oracle@aks02 admin]$
[oracle@aks02 admin]$
[oracle@aks02 admin]$ cat listener.ora
LISTENER =
  (DESCRIPTION_LIST =
    (DESCRIPTION =
      (ADDRESS = (PROTOCOL = TCP)(HOST = aks02.dbagenesis.com)(PORT = 1521))
    )
  )

SID_LIST_LISTENER =
  (SID_LIST =
    (SID_DESC =
      (GLOBAL_DBNAME = CDB_STB_DGMGRL)
      (ORACLE_HOME = /u01/app/oracle/product/19.3/db_home)
      (SID_NAME = CDB)
    )
  )

ADR_BASE_LISTENER = /u01/app/oracle
[oracle@aks02 admin]$
```

CHAPTER 4

Perform Manual Switchover

Perform Manual Switchover on Physical Standby

https://support.dbagenesis.com/post/oracle-data-guard-manual-switchover-and-failover-on-physical-standby#viewer-9csu1

On Primary Server

```
sqlplus sys/sys@proddb as sysdba

select name, open_mode, db_unique_name, database_role from v$database;

NAME      OPEN_MODE      DB_UNIQUE_NAME         DATABASE_ROLE
--------- -------------- ----------------------
--------------
proddb    READ WRITE     proddb                 PRIMARY
```

```
[oracle@aks01 admin]$ sqlplus / as sysdba

SQL*Plus: Release 19.0.0.0.0 - Production on Sat May 25 12:49:49 2024
Version 19.3.0.0.0

Copyright (c) 1982, 2019, Oracle.  All rights reserved.


Connected to:
Oracle Database 19c Enterprise Edition Release 19.0.0.0.0 - Production
Version 19.3.0.0.0

SQL>
SQL>
SQL> select name, open_mode, db_unique_name, database_role from v$database;

NAME      OPEN_MODE            DB_UNIQUE_NAME                 DATABASE_ROLE
--------- -------------------- ------------------------------ ----------------
CDB       READ WRITE           CDB                            PRIMARY

SQL>
```

Check primary and standby for any gaps

On Primary Server:

```
select STATUS, GAP_STATUS from
V$ARCHIVE_DEST_STATUS where DEST_ID = 2;
```

On Primary Server

```
SQL>
SQL> select STATUS, GAP_STATUS from V$ARCHIVE_DEST_STATUS where DEST_ID = 2;

STATUS    GAP_STATUS
--------- ------------------------
VALID     NO GAP

SQL>
```

On Standby Server

```
select NAME, VALUE, DATUM_TIME from
V$DATAGUARD_STATS;
```

```
[oracle@aks02 admin]$ sqlplus / as sysdba

SQL*Plus: Release 19.0.0.0.0 - Production on Sat May 25 12:51:02 2024
Version 19.3.0.0.0

Copyright (c) 1982, 2019, Oracle.  All rights reserved.


Connected to:
Oracle Database 19c Enterprise Edition Release 19.0.0.0.0 - Production
Version 19.3.0.0.0

SQL>
```

```
NAME                              VALUE
--------------------------------- ----------------
------
transport lag                     +00 00:00:00
apply lag                         +00 00:00:00
apply finish time                 +00 00:00:00.000
estimated startup time            7

SQL>
```

We will first convert primary to standby and later standby to primary.

On Primary Server

```
select SWITCHOVER_STATUS from V$DATABASE;
```

```
SQL> select SWITCHOVER_STATUS from V$DATABASE;

SWITCHOVER_STATUS
--------------------
TO STANDBY

SQL>
```

You must see **TO STANDBY** or **SESSIONS ACTIVE**

```
alter database commit to switchover to
physical standby with session shutdown;
startup mount;
```

```
SQL> alter database commit to switchover to physical standby with session shutdown;

Database altered.

SQL> startup mount;
ORACLE instance started.

Total System Global Area 1577055360 bytes
Fixed Size                   9135232 bytes
Variable Size              385875968 bytes
Database Buffers          1174405120 bytes
Redo Buffers                 7639040 bytes
Database mounted.
SQL>
```

Convert standby to primary: Our primary is already converted to standby. Now it's time to convert original standby into primary

On Standby Server

```
select SWITCHOVER_STATUS from V$DATABASE;

alter database commit to switchover to
primary with session shutdown;

alter database open;
```

```
SQL> select SWITCHOVER_STATUS from V$DATABASE;

SWITCHOVER_STATUS
--------------------
TO PRIMARY

SQL> alter database commit to switchover to primary with session shutdown;

Database altered.

SQL> alter database open;

Database altered.

SQL>
```

At this stage, the client query would execute successfully!

On new standby – Initially your primary database: Start MRP

```
alter database recover managed standby
database disconnect;
```

On Primary Server

```
SQL> alter database recover managed standby database disconnect;

Database altered.

SQL>
SQL>
SQL> select process, status, sequence# from v$managed_standby;

PROCESS   STATUS       SEQUENCE#
--------- ------------ ----------
ARCH      CONNECTED             0
DGRD      ALLOCATED             0
DGRD      ALLOCATED             0
ARCH      CONNECTED             0
RFS       IDLE                  0
ARCH      CLOSING              46
ARCH      CONNECTED             0
RFS       IDLE                 47
RFS       IDLE                  0
MRP0      APPLYING_LOG         47

10 rows selected.

SQL>
```

On Standby Server

```
SQL> archive log list;
Database log mode              Archive Mode
Automatic archival             Enabled
Archive destination            USE_DB_RECOVERY_FILE_DEST
Oldest online log sequence     46
Next log sequence to archive   47
Current log sequence           47
SQL>
```

```
SQL> alter system switch logfile;

System altered.

SQL> /

System altered.

SQL> /

System altered.

SQL> /

System altered.

SQL>
```

On Primary Server

```
SQL> /

PROCESS   STATUS        SEQUENCE#
--------- ------------ ----------
ARCH      CONNECTED             0
DGRD      ALLOCATED             0
DGRD      ALLOCATED             0
ARCH      CLOSING              50
RFS       IDLE                  0
ARCH      CLOSING              46
ARCH      CLOSING              49
RFS       IDLE                 51
RFS       IDLE                  0
MRP0      APPLYING_LOG         51

10 rows selected.

SQL>
```

Revert back: Once again follow the above process from top and re-execute steps in proper databases to revert back to original setup.

On Standby Server

```
SQL> select STATUS, GAP_STATUS from V$ARCHIVE_DEST_STATUS where DEST_ID = 2;

STATUS    GAP_STATUS
--------- ------------------------
VALID     NO GAP

SQL>
```

On Primary Server

```
SQL> select NAME, VALUE, DATUM_TIME from V$DATAGUARD_STATS;
```

```
NAME                                VALUE
----------------------------------- -----------
------
transport lag                       +00 00:00:00
apply lag                           +00 00:00:00
apply finish time
estimated startup time              7

SQL>
```

On Standby Server

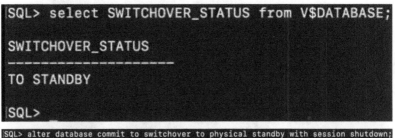

```
SQL> select SWITCHOVER_STATUS from V$DATABASE;

SWITCHOVER_STATUS
--------------------
TO STANDBY

SQL>
```

```
SQL> alter database commit to switchover to physical standby with session shutdown;

Database altered.

SQL>
```

```
SQL> startup mount;
ORACLE instance started.

Total System Global Area 1577055360 bytes
Fixed Size                  9135232 bytes
Variable Size             385875968 bytes
Database Buffers         1174405120 bytes
Redo Buffers                7639040 bytes

Database mounted.
```

On Primary Server

```
SQL> select SWITCHOVER_STATUS from V$DATABASE;

SWITCHOVER_STATUS
--------------------
TO PRIMARY

SQL> alter database commit to switchover to primary with session shutdown;

Database altered.

SQL> alter database open;

Database altered.

SQL>
```

On Standby Server

```
SQL> alter database recover managed standby database disconnect;

Database altered.

SQL>
```

CHAPTER 5

Snapshot Standby

Opening physical standby for testing purposes and reverting back is known as Snapshot Standby.

Steps for Snapshot Standby

```
Physical Standby
     - MRP - applying logs
     - Mount


Snapshot Standby
     - Stop MRP
     - Create Restore Point (Stb -> Snap Stb)
     - Open the DB

     - Connect to standby & test your code


Convert back to Physical Standby
     - Move back to Restore Point
     - Put DB in mount Mode
     - Start MRP
```

Convert Physical Standby into Snapshot Standby
https://support.dbagenesis.com/post/convert-physical-standby-into-snapshot-standby

One of the most powerful features of Oracle Data Guard is Snapshot Standby. Let's assume that the application team wants to test something on production data. Rather than cloning prod, we can convert existing physical standby into snapshot standby, perform the testing and convert it back to physical standby.

We can always revert back snapshot standby to the point when it was converted to snapshot standby from physical standby. This way we can repeat the cycle any number of times, perform testing, convert back to physical standby and sync back again with production.

Convert physical standby to snapshot standby: We will now convert the physical standby database to snapshot standby.

On Standby Server

```
SQL> alter database recover managed standby
database cancel;
SQL> select name, open_mode from v$database;
SQL> alter database convert to snapshot
standby;
SQL> alter database open;
SQL> select name, open_mode, database_role
from v$database;
```

```
SQL> alter database recover managed standby database cancel;

Database altered.

SQL> select process, status, sequence# from v$managed_standby;

PROCESS   STATUS       SEQUENCE#
--------- ------------ ----------
ARCH      CONNECTED             0
DGRD      ALLOCATED             0
DGRD      ALLOCATED             0
ARCH      CONNECTED             0
ARCH      CLOSING              52
ARCH      CONNECTED             0
RFS       IDLE                  0
RFS       IDLE                 53
RFS       IDLE                  0

9 rows selected.
```

```
SQL> select name, open_mode from v$database;

NAME      OPEN_MODE
--------- --------------------
CDB       MOUNTED

SQL> alter database convert to snapshot standby;

Database altered.

SQL> alter database open;

Database altered.
```

```
SQL> select name, open_mode, database_role from v$database;

NAME      OPEN_MODE            DATABASE_ROLE
--------- -------------------- ----------------
CDB       READ WRITE           SNAPSHOT STANDBY

SQL>
```

Verifying snapshot standby: Now you must be able to read-write on snapshot standby. Meanwhile, we can even check the standby alert log. The archives received from primary are not applied on standby. We can even check that there is a guaranteed restore point has been created. So that when you convert the snapshot back to physical standby, it will be used.

On Standby Server

```
SQL> select name,
guarantee_flashback_database from
v$restore_point;
SQL> create table student(sno number(2),
s_name varchar2(10));
SQL> insert into student values(1,'RAM');
SQL> insert into student values (2,'Max');
SQL> commit;
SQL> select * from student;
```

```
SQL> select name, guarantee_flashback_database from v$restore_point;

NAME
GUA
--------------------------------------------------------------------------------
------ ---
SNAPSHOT_STANDBY_REQUIRED_05/25/2024 13:24:36
YES
```

```
SQL> create table student(sno number(2), s_name varchar2(10));

Table created.

SQL>
SQL> insert into student values(1,'RAM');

1 row created.

SQL> insert into student values(1,'RAM');

1 row created.

SQL> insert into student values(1,'RAM');

1 row created.

SQL>
SQL>
SQL> commit;

Commit complete.

SQL>
SQL> select * from student
  2  ;

       SNO S_NAME
---------- ----------
         1 RAM
         1 RAM
         1 RAM

SQL>
```

On Primary Server

```
SQL> archive log list;
Database log mode              Archive Mode
Automatic archival             Enabled
Archive destination            USE_DB_RECOVERY_FILE_DEST
Oldest online log sequence     52
Next log sequence to archive   53
Current log sequence           53
SQL>
SQL>
SQL>
SQL> alter system switch logfile;

System altered.

SQL> /

System altered.

SQL> /
```

Revert back snapshot standby to physical standby: Once application testing is done, you can revert back snapshot standby to the same point when it was converted from physical standby to snapshot standby.

On Standby Server

```
SQL> select name, open_mode, database_role
from v$database;
SQL> shut immediate;
SQL> startup mount;
SQL> alter database convert to physical
standby;
SQL> alter database recover managed standby
database disconnect;
SQL> select * from student;
```

```
SQL> select name, open_mode, database_role from v$database;

NAME      OPEN_MODE            DATABASE_ROLE
--------- -------------------- ----------------
CDB       READ WRITE           SNAPSHOT STANDBY

SQL>
SQL>
SQL>
SQL> shut immediate;

Database closed.
Database dismounted.
ORACLE instance shut down.
```

```
SQL> startup mount;
ORACLE instance started.

Total System Global Area 1577055360 bytes
Fixed Size                  9135232 bytes
Variable Size             385875968 bytes
Database Buffers         1174405120 bytes
Redo Buffers                7639040 bytes
Database mounted.
SQL>
SQL>
SQL> alter database convert to physical standby;

Database altered.
```

```
SQL> alter database recover managed standby database disconnect;

Database altered.

SQL> select process, status, sequence# from v$managed_standby;

PROCESS   STATUS        SEQUENCE#
--------- ------------ ----------
ARCH      CONNECTED             0
DGRD      ALLOCATED             0
DGRD      ALLOCATED             0
ARCH      CLOSING              53
ARCH      CONNECTED             0
ARCH      CONNECTED             0
RFS       IDLE                  0
RFS       IDLE                 56
MRP0      APPLYING_LOG         56

9 rows selected.
```

On Primary Server

```
SQL> archive log list;
Database log mode              Archive Mode
Automatic archival             Enabled
Archive destination            USE_DB_RECOVERY_FILE_DEST
Oldest online log sequence     54
Next log sequence to archive   56
Current log sequence           56
SQL>
```

When do you think you can use Snapshot Standby?

If you receive a request to clone a primary database for short-term testing (one or two days), first check if there is a standby configured for that primary. If there is, use the physical standby, convert it into a snapshot, complete the testing, and then revert it back.

Assignments

1. Try Manual Failover
2. Try Active Data Guard

CHAPTER 6

Active Data Guard

Active Data Guard is a feature of Oracle Database that allows the physical standby database to be open for read-only and reporting operations while continuously applying changes from the primary database in real-time.

In simple terms, when you open a Physical Standby in read-only mode, it is known as Active Data Guard. However, Active Data Guard requires a license, so you should check with Oracle before implementing it.

Enable Active Data Guard - On Standby Server

```
SQL> alter database recover managed standby
database cancel;
SQL> alter database open;
SQL> select name, open_mode, database_role
from v$database;
SQL> alter database recover managed standby
database disconnect;
```

```
SQL> alter database recover managed standby database cancel;

Database altered.

SQL> select name, open_mode, database_role from v$database;

NAME      OPEN_MODE            DATABASE_ROLE
--------- -------------------- ----------------
CDB       MOUNTED              PHYSICAL STANDBY

SQL>
SQL> alter database open;

Database altered.
```

```
SQL> alter database open;

Database altered.

SQL> select name, open_mode, database_role from v$database;

NAME      OPEN_MODE            DATABASE_ROLE
--------- -------------------- ----------------
CDB       READ ONLY            PHYSICAL STANDBY

SQL> alter database recover managed standby database disconnect;

Database altered.
```

If we open physical standby for read only and still have an MRP process running in the background is known as Active Data Guard.

```
SQL> select process, status, sequence# from v$managed_standby;

PROCESS   STATUS       SEQUENCE#
--------- ------------ ----------
ARCH      CLOSING              56
DGRD      ALLOCATED             0
DGRD      ALLOCATED             0
ARCH      CLOSING              53
ARCH      CONNECTED             0
ARCH      CLOSING              57
RFS       IDLE                  0
RFS       IDLE                 58
MRP0      APPLYING_LOG         58

9 rows selected.
```

On Primary Server

```
SQL> archive log list;
Database log mode              Archive Mode
Automatic archival             Enabled
Archive destination            USE_DB_RECOVERY_FILE_DEST
Oldest online log sequence     56
Next log sequence to archive   58
Current log sequence           58
SQL>
SQL>
SQL>
SQL> alter system switch logfile;

System altered.

SQL> /

System altered.
```

On Standby Server

```
SQL> select process, status, sequence# from v$managed_standby;
```

```
PROCESS   STATUS       SEQUENCE#
--------- ------------ ----------
ARCH      CLOSING              59
DGRD      ALLOCATED             0
DGRD      ALLOCATED             0
ARCH      CLOSING              53
ARCH      CLOSING              58
ARCH      CLOSING              57
RFS       IDLE                  0
RFS       IDLE                 60
MRP0      APPLYING_LOG         60
```

Revert back to physical standby

If you want to convert active data guard back to physical standby, follow below commands.

On Standby Server

```
SQL> alter database recover managed standby database cancel;
SQL> shutdown immediate;
SQL> startup mount;
SQL> select name, open_mode, database_role from v$database;
SQL> alter database recover managed standby database disconnect;
SQL> select process, status, sequence# from v$managed_standby;
```

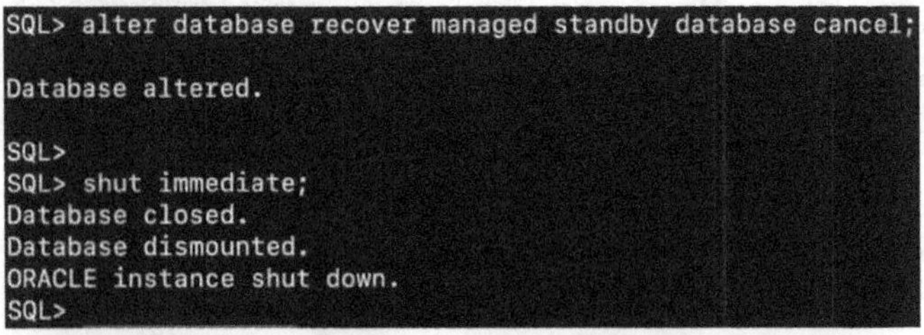

```
SQL> alter database recover managed standby database cancel;

Database altered.

SQL>
SQL> shut immediate;
Database closed.
Database dismounted.
ORACLE instance shut down.
SQL>
```

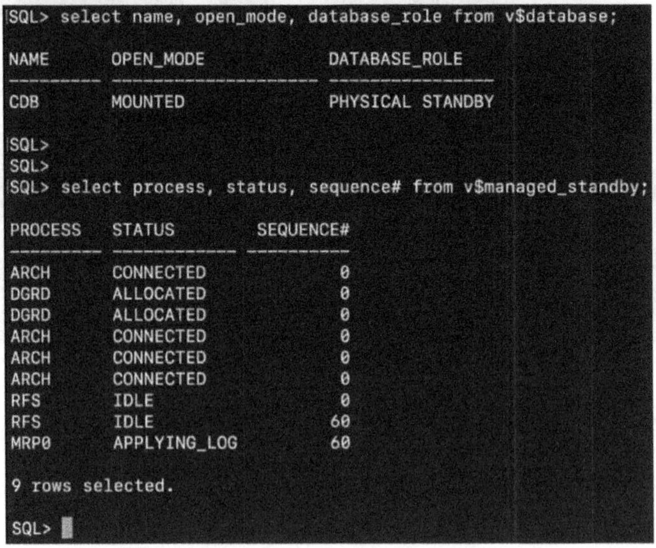

```
SQL> select name, open_mode, database_role from v$database;

NAME      OPEN_MODE            DATABASE_ROLE
--------- -------------------- ----------------
CDB       MOUNTED              PHYSICAL STANDBY

SQL>
SQL>
SQL> select process, status, sequence# from v$managed_standby;

PROCESS   STATUS        SEQUENCE#
--------- ------------ ----------
ARCH      CONNECTED             0
DGRD      ALLOCATED             0
DGRD      ALLOCATED             0
ARCH      CONNECTED             0
ARCH      CONNECTED             0
ARCH      CONNECTED             0
RFS       IDLE                  0
RFS       IDLE                 60
MRP0      APPLYING_LOG         60

9 rows selected.

SQL>
```

Active Data Guard is commonly used in environments with a high volume of SELECT operations. If your workload primarily involves INSERT, UPDATE, and DELETE operations, a physical standby is usually preferred. However, if you have a reporting team that needs to run queries for quality analysis or other purposes, Active Data Guard is the better choice.

CHAPTER 7

Perform Manual Failover

Failover is when your primary database is completely lost. When there is a failover, standby is converted into primary but primary is not converted into standby as it is lost. If you do not have Flashback enabled on primary, you must recreate primary from scratch (Using RMAN duplicate method). In this example, we have already enabled flashback on both primary and standby.

Crash Primary database

Let's crash primary: In order to simulate failure, we will shut down the primary server.

On Primary Server

```
SQL> exit
Disconnected from Oracle Database 19c Enterprise Edition Release 19.0.0.0.0 - Production
Version 19.3.0.0.0


[oracle@aks01 ~]$
[oracle@aks01 ~]$
[oracle@aks01 ~]$
[oracle@aks01 ~]$
[oracle@aks01 ~]$
[oracle@aks01 ~]$ exit
logout
[root@aks01 ~]#
[root@aks01 ~]#
[root@aks01 ~]#
[root@aks01 ~]# reboot
Connection to 65.109.170.250 closed by remote host.
Connection to 65.109.170.250 closed.
taff@Taffs-MacBook-Pro sshKeys %
```

Execute query on client: At this stage, there is no primary to accept queries from client. Run below query on client putty terminal. The query will hang and wait until standby is converted to primary.

```
select name, open_mode, db_unique_name,
database_role from v$database;
```

Perform Failover to Standby

Minimize data loss: If you can mount the primary database, then flush the logs to standby.

On Primary Server

```
SQL> startup mount
SQL> alter system flush redo to 'proddb_st';
```

If you are not able to mount the database, then check if the primary server is up. In that case manually copy archive logs from primary to standby and register those logs on standby database.

On Standby Server:

```
SQL> alter database register physical
logfile '&logfile_path';
```

Check for redo gaps: If any gap exists, copy log files from primary and register on standby as per last step

On Standby Server

```
SQL> select THREAD#, LOW_SEQUENCE#,
HIGH_SEQUENCE# from V$ARCHIVE_GAP;
```

Start failover: We need to activate standby so that client can continue to access even after failover

On Standby Server

```
SQL> ALTER DATABASE RECOVER MANAGED STANDBY
DATABASE CANCEL;
SQL> ALTER DATABASE RECOVER MANAGED STANDBY
DATABASE FINISH;
SQL> select SWITCHOVER_STATUS from
V$DATABASE;
```

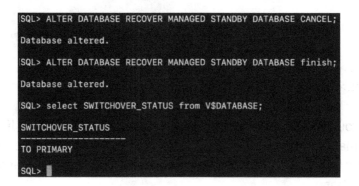

```
SQL> ALTER DATABASE RECOVER MANAGED STANDBY DATABASE CANCEL;

Database altered.

SQL> ALTER DATABASE RECOVER MANAGED STANDBY DATABASE finish;

Database altered.

SQL> select SWITCHOVER_STATUS from V$DATABASE;

SWITCHOVER_STATUS
--------------------
TO PRIMARY

SQL>
```

You must see TO PRIMARY or SESSIONS ACTIVE. Switch standby to primary

```
SQL> alter database commit to switchover to
primary with session shutdown;
SQL> alter database open;
```

```
SQL> alter database commit to switchover to primary with session shutdown;

Database altered.

SQL> alter database open;

Database altered.

SQL>
```

Check client query: Check the query you executed in step 2 on client, it must get executed.

Rebuild Primary After Failover

Post failover, there are two methods of rebuilding your failed primary

- **Method 1:** Rebuild from scratch using RMAN duplicate
- **Method 2:** Flashback database only if Flashback was enabled

Get the SCN at which standby became primary: We need to get the SCN at which the current primary (proddb_st) was activated. This SCN will be used to flashback crashed (proddb) database

On Standby Server

```
SQL> select
to_char(standby_became_primary_scn) from
v$database;
```

```
SQL> select to_char(standby_became_primary_scn) from v$database;

TO_CHAR(STANDBY_BECAME_PRIMARY_SCN)
----------------------------------------
3736535

SQL>
```

On Primary Server

```
taff@Taffs-MacBook-Pro sshKeys %
taff@Taffs-MacBook-Pro sshKeys % ssh -i dbagenesisCloudConnectKey.pem root@65.109.170.250
Enter passphrase for key 'dbagenesisCloudConnectKey.pem':
Last login: Mon May 27 13:05:42 2024 from 183.82.112.100
-bash: warning: setlocale: LC_CTYPE: cannot change locale (UTF-8): No such file or directory
[root@aks01 ~]#
[root@aks01 ~]#
[root@aks01 ~]#
[root@aks01 ~]# su - oracle
Last login: Mon May 27 13:05:52 CEST 2024 on pts/1
[oracle@aks01 ~]$
[oracle@aks01 ~]$
[oracle@aks01 ~]$
[oracle@aks01 ~]$ sqlplus / as sysdba

SQL*Plus: Release 19.0.0.0.0 - Production on Mon May 27 13:18:05 2024
Version 19.3.0.0.0

Copyright (c) 1982, 2019, Oracle.  All rights reserved.

Connected to an idle instance.

SQL>
```

Flashback crashed primary : Start the Primary server, mount the database and flashback primary server to SCN from the last step

```
SQL> startup mount;
SQL> flashback database to scn
<standby_became_primary_scn>;
```

```
SQL> startup mount;
ORACLE instance started.

Total System Global Area 1577055360 bytes
Fixed Size                  9135232 bytes
Variable Size             385875968 bytes
Database Buffers         1174405120 bytes
Redo Buffers                7639040 bytes
Database mounted.
SQL>
SQL>
SQL>
SQL>
SQL> flashback database to scn 3736535;

Flashback complete.

SQL>
```

Convert crashed primary to physical standby: Now the old primary is at SCN when the primary server was activated. We can convert primary server into a physical standby and start redo apply

```
SQL> alter database convert to physical standby;
SQL> alter database recover managed standby database disconnect;
```

```
SQL> alter database convert to physical standby;

Database altered.

SQL> alter database recover managed standby database disconnect;

Database altered.

SQL>
```

On Standby Server

```
SQL> archive log list;
Database log mode              Archive Mode
Automatic archival             Enabled
Archive destination            USE_DB_RECOVERY_FILE_DEST
Oldest online log sequence     1
Next log sequence to archive   2
Current log sequence           2
SQL>
```

On Primary Server

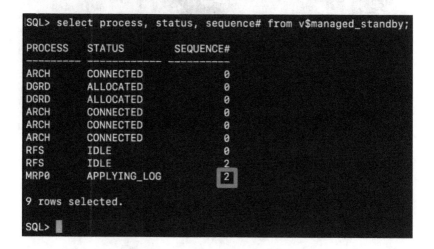

```
SQL> select process, status, sequence# from v$managed_standby;

PROCESS   STATUS       SEQUENCE#
--------- ------------ ----------
ARCH      CONNECTED             0
DGRD      ALLOCATED             0
DGRD      ALLOCATED             0
ARCH      CONNECTED             0
ARCH      CONNECTED             0
ARCH      CONNECTED             0
RFS       IDLE                  0
RFS       IDLE                  2
MRP0      APPLYING_LOG          2

9 rows selected.

SQL>
```

We can see on the standby server, archive log sequences are reset if we open the standby server.

Revert to original configuration: At this stage, if you would like to revert the current state of databases to original, you can perform manual switchover.

On Standby Server

```
[oracle@aks02 ~]$ sqlplus / as sysdba

SQL*Plus: Release 19.0.0.0.0 - Production on Mon May 27 13:30:38 2024
Version 19.3.0.0.0

Copyright (c) 1982, 2019, Oracle.  All rights reserved.


Connected to:
Oracle Database 19c Enterprise Edition Release 19.0.0.0.0 - Production
Version 19.3.0.0.0

SQL> select STATUS, GAP_STATUS from V$ARCHIVE_DEST_STATUS where DEST_ID = 2;

STATUS    GAP_STATUS
--------- ------------------------
VALID     NO GAP

SQL>
```

```
SQL> alter database commit to switchover to physical standby with session shutdown;

Database altered.

SQL> startup mount;
ORACLE instance started.

Total System Global Area 1577055360 bytes
Fixed Size                  9135232 bytes
Variable Size             385875968 bytes
Database Buffers         1174405120 bytes
Redo Buffers                7639040 bytes
Database mounted.
SQL>
```

On Primary Server

```
SQL> select SWITCHOVER_STATUS from V$DATABASE;

SWITCHOVER_STATUS
--------------------
TO PRIMARY

SQL>
SQL> alter database commit to switchover to primary with session shutdown;

Database altered.

SQL>
SQL> alter database open;

Database altered.

SQL>
```

On Standby Server

```
SQL> alter database recover managed standby database disconnect;

Database altered.

SQL>
```

CHAPTER 8

Data Guard Broker

Data Guard Protection Modes

https://support.dbagenesis.com/post/oracle-data-guard-protection-modes

A Data Guard configuration always runs in one of three data protection modes (also called Redo Transport rules).

1. Maximum Performance
2. Maximum Availability
3. Maximum Protection

Mode	Redo transport	Action with no standby database connection	Risk of data loss
Maximum Protection	SYNC and LGWR	The primary database needs to write redo to at least one standby database. Otherwise it will shut down.	Zero data loss is guaranteed.
Maximum Availability	SYNC and LGWR	Normally works with SYNC redo transport. If the primary database cannot write redo to any of its standby databases, it continues processing transactions as in ASYNC mode.	Zero data loss in normal operation, but not guaranteed.
Maximum Performance	ASYNC and LGWR/ARCH	Never expects acknowledgment from the standby database.	Potential for minimal data loss in a normal operation.

- By default, the protection mode is **MAX PERFORMANCE**. If you look above, MAX PERFORMANCE uses ASYNC redo transport and rest other protection modes use SYNC protection mode.

- Also, looking at **MAX PROTECTION** and **MAX AVAILABILITY**, we can say that the **MAX PROTECTION** mode is not used in real time. The main reason is if standby is unavailable, primary will shut down.

- The ultimate protection modes you must use are: **MAX PERFORMANCE and MAX AVAILABILITY.**

How do we change Data Guard Protection modes?

Mostly we have redo transport async and sync. Async means primary will not wait for acknowledgement from standby that the redo or archive has been applied. Sync means our primary will wait for standby to send the reply that the transaction has been applied.

Inside our database, how do we check which protection mode are we in?

On Primary Server

```
select protection_mode from v$database;
```

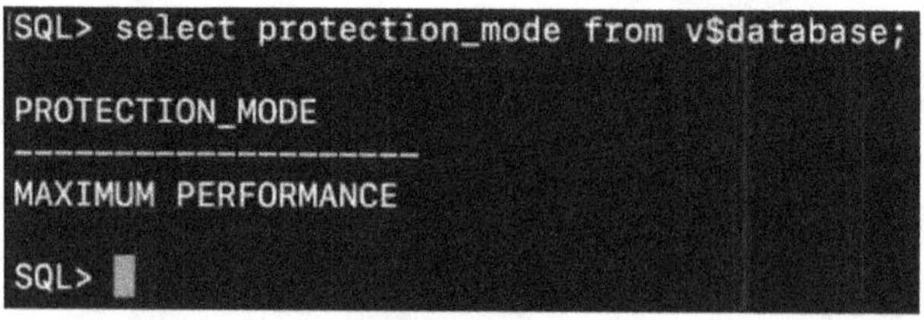

Switch from Max Performance to Max Availability Protection Mode

Verify the broker configuration, check if it's enabled and make sure log apply is enabled

```
dgmgrl sys/oracle@proddb

show configuration
show database proddb
show database proddb_st
edit database proddb_st set state=apply-on;
```

Change LNS mode from ASYN to SYNC

```
EDIT DATABASE proddb_st SET PROPERTY
LogXptMode='SYNC';
EDIT CONFIGURATION SET PROTECTION MODE AS
MaxAvailability;
```

Switch from Max Availability to Max Performance Protection Mode

Verify the broker configuration, check if it's enabled and make sure log apply is enabled

```
dgmgrl sys/oracle@proddb

show configuration
show database proddb
show database proddb_st
edit database proddb_st set state=apply-on;
```

Change LNS mode from ASYN to SYNC

```
EDIT DATABASE proddb_st SET PROPERTY
LogXptMode='ASYNC';
EDIT CONFIGURATION SET PROTECTION MODE AS
MaxPerformance;
```

Oracle Data Guard Broker

We spend a lot of time configuring Data Guard manually. Can we automate the setup, switchover, and failover processes? For a new setup, doing all of this manually can be a headache. Fortunately, Oracle has already automated these tasks for us with a tool called the Data Guard Broker.

We can set up a data guard in two ways:

1. Manual Method
2. Data Guard Broker

Difference between Manual Method and Data Guard Broker

The difference is all about redo transport.

Oracle Data Guard Physical Standby Configuration
https://support.dbagenesis.com/post/oracle-data-guard-physical-standby-configuration

If we want to convert manual setup into data guard broker, we need to perform only one change i.e. Disable redo transport.

On Primary Server

```
SQL> alter system set log_archive_dest_2='';

System altered.

SQL>
```

On Standby Server

```
SQL> alter system set log_archive_dest_2='';

System altered.

SQL>
```

Enable Data Guard Broker

At this point we have a primary database and a standby database, so now we need to start using the Data Guard Broker to manage them. Connect to both databases (primary and standby) and issue the following command.

On Primary Server

```
SQL> show parameter dg_broker_start;
SQL> alter system set dg_broker_start=TRUE;
```

```
SQL> show parameter dg_broker_start;

NAME                                 TYPE        VALUE
------------------------------------ ----------- ------
dg_broker_start                      boolean     FALSE
SQL>
SQL> alter system set dg_broker_start=TRUE;

System altered.

SQL>
```

On Standby Server

```
SQL> alter system set dg_broker_start=TRUE;
SQL> show parameter dg_broker_start;
```

```
SQL> alter system set dg_broker_start=TRUE;

System altered.

SQL>
SQL> show parameter dg_broker_start;

NAME                                 TYPE        VALUE
------------------------------------ ----------- ------
dg_broker_start                      boolean     TRUE
SQL>
```

On primary, connect to DGMGRL utility and register the primary database with broker

On Primary Server

```
dgmgrl sys@ip7
DGMGRL> create configuration CDB_DR as
primary database is CDB connect identifier
is CDB;
DGMGRL> show configuration;
```

```
SQL> exit
Disconnected from Oracle Database 19c Enterprise Edition Release 19.0.0.0.0 - Production
Version 19.3.0.0.0


[oracle@aks01 ~]$
[oracle@aks01 ~]$
[oracle@aks01 ~]$ dgmgrl sys@CDB
DGMGRL for Linux: Release 19.0.0.0.0 - Production on Tue May 28 13:17:06 2024
Version 19.3.0.0.0

Copyright (c) 1982, 2019, Oracle and/or its affiliates.  All rights reserved.

Welcome to DGMGRL, type "help" for information.
Password:
Connected to "CDB"
Connected as SYSDBA.
DGMGRL>
```

```
DGMGRL> create configuration CDB_DR as primary database is CDB connect identifier is CDB;
Configuration "cdb_dr" created with primary database "cdb"
DGMGRL>
DGMGRL> show configuration;

Configuration - cdb_dr

  Protection Mode: MaxPerformance
  Members:
  cdb - Primary database

Fast-Start Failover:  Disabled

Configuration Status:
DISABLED

DGMGRL>
```

Now add standby database

```
DGMGRL> add database CDB_STB as connect
identifier is CDB_STB;
DGMGRL> show configuration;
```

```
DGMGRL> add database CDB_STB as connect identifier is CDB_STB;
Database "cdb_stb" added
DGMGRL>
DGMGRL>
DGMGRL> show configuration;

Configuration - cdb_dr

  Protection Mode: MaxPerformance
  Members:
  cdb     - Primary database
    cdb_stb - Physical standby database

Fast-Start Failover:  Disabled

Configuration Status:
DISABLED

DGMGRL>
DGMGRL> ENABLE CONFIGURATION;
Enabled.
DGMGRL>
```

Enable configuration

```
DGMGRL> ENABLE CONFIGURATION;
```

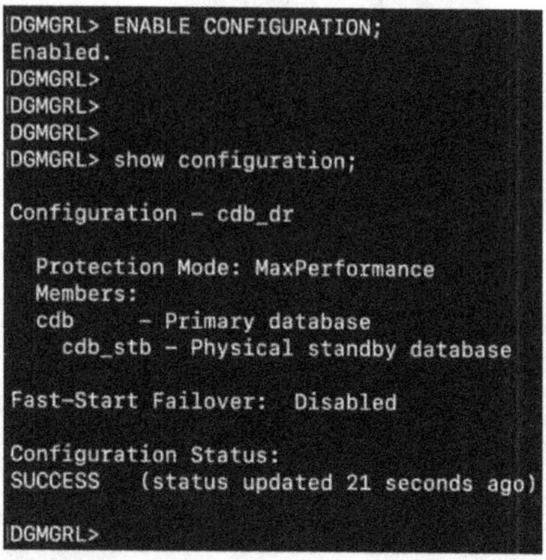

```
DGMGRL> ENABLE CONFIGURATION;
Enabled.
DGMGRL>
DGMGRL>
DGMGRL>
DGMGRL> show configuration;

Configuration - cdb_dr

  Protection Mode: MaxPerformance
  Members:
  cdb     - Primary database
    cdb_stb - Physical standby database

Fast-Start Failover:  Disabled

Configuration Status:
SUCCESS   (status updated 21 seconds ago)

DGMGRL>
```

The following commands demonstrate how to check the configuration and status of the databases using the Data Guard Broker. Similar to manually starting or stopping the MRP, you can start or stop redo apply on the standby using the broker.

Stop log apply

```
DGMGRL> show configuration;
DGMGRL> show database cdb;
DGMGRL> show database cdb_stb;
DGMGRL> edit database cbd set
state=APPLY-OFF;
DGMGRL> show database cdb;
```

```
DGMGRL> show configuration;

Configuration - cdb_dr

  Protection Mode: MaxPerformance
  Members:
  cdb     - Primary database
    cdb_stb - Physical standby database

Fast-Start Failover:  Disabled

Configuration Status:
SUCCESS   (status updated 21 seconds ago)

DGMGRL>
```

```
DGMGRL> show database cdb;

Database - cdb

  Role:               PRIMARY
  Intended State:     TRANSPORT-ON
  Instance(s):
    CDB

Database Status:
SUCCESS

DGMGRL>
DGMGRL>
```

```
DGMGRL> show database cdb_stb

Database - cdb_stb

  Role:                  PHYSICAL STANDBY
  Intended State:        APPLY-ON
  Transport Lag:         0 seconds (computed 0 seconds ago)
  Apply Lag:             0 seconds (computed 0 seconds ago)
  Average Apply Rate: 2.00 KByte/s
  Real Time Query:       OFF
  Instance(s):
    CDB

Database Status:
SUCCESS

DGMGRL>
```

```
DGMGRL> edit database cdb set state=TRANSPORT-OFF;
Succeeded.
```

```
DGMGRL> show database cdb;

Database - cdb

  Role:                  PRIMARY
  Intended State:        TRANSPORT-OFF
  Instance(s):
    CDB

Database Status:
SUCCESS

DGMGRL>
```

Start log apply

```
DGMGRL> edit database cdb set
state=TRANSPORT-ON;
DGMGRL> show database cdb;
```

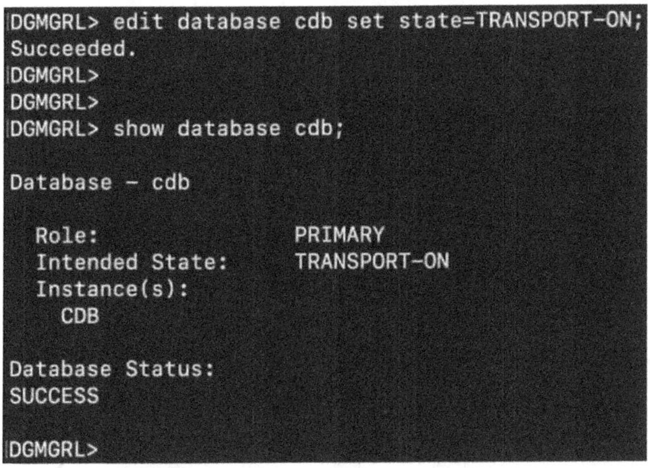

```
DGMGRL> edit database cdb set state=TRANSPORT-ON;
Succeeded.
DGMGRL>
DGMGRL>
DGMGRL> show database cdb;

Database - cdb

  Role:               PRIMARY
  Intended State:     TRANSPORT-ON
  Instance(s):
    CDB

Database Status:
SUCCESS

DGMGRL>
```

Data Guard Broker Switchover
https://support.dbagenesis.com/post/oracle-data-guard-broker-switchover-and-failover#viewer-8e3kv

On the Primary server

```
DGMGRL> show configuration;
DGMGRL> switchover to cdb_stb;
```

```
DGMGRL> show configuration

Configuration - cdb_dr

  Protection Mode: MaxPerformance
  Members:
  cdb     - Primary database
    cdb_stb - Physical standby database

Fast-Start Failover:  Disabled

Configuration Status:
SUCCESS   (status updated 53 seconds ago)

DGMGRL>
```

```
DGMGRL> switchover to cdb_stb;
Performing switchover NOW, please wait...
Operation requires a connection to database "cdb_stb"
Connecting ...
Connected to "CDB_STB"
Connected as SYSDBA.
New primary database "cdb_stb" is opening...
Operation requires start up of instance "CDB" on database "cdb"
Starting instance "CDB"...
Connected to an idle instance.
ORACLE instance started.
Connected to "CDB"
Database mounted.
Connected to "CDB"
Switchover succeeded, new primary is "cdb_stb"
DGMGRL>
```

```
DGMGRL> show configuration;

Configuration - cdb_dr

  Protection Mode: MaxPerformance
  Members:
  cdb_stb - Primary database
    cdb     - Physical standby database

Fast-Start Failover:  Disabled

Configuration Status:
SUCCESS   (status updated 78 seconds ago)

DGMGRL>
```

Assignment

- **Data Guard Broker Failover**
  https://support.dbagenesis.com/post/oracle-data-guard-broker-switchover-and-failover#viewer-2fffr

CHAPTER 9

Projects

Projects

1. Enable the real-time apply
2. Convert standby into logical standby
3. Configure Cascading DR
4. Convert Physical standby into logical standby https://support.dbagenesis.com/post/convert-physical-standby-into-logical-standby

Thank you!

Your comments encourage us to produce quality content, please take a second and say 'Hi' to me and let me and my team know what you thought of the book … p.s. It would mean the world to me if you send a quick email to me ;)

Email: support@dbagenesis.com
Link to full course: https://dbagenesis.com/
Link to all DBA courses: https://dbagenesis.com/courses
Link to support articles: https://support.dbagenesis.com

DBA Genesis provides all you need to build and manage effective Oracle technology learning. We designed DBA Genesis as a simple to use yet powerful online Oracle learning system for students. Each of our courses is taught by an expert instructor, and every course is available with a challenging project to push you out of your comfort zone!!

DBA Genesis is currently the fastest & the most engaging learning platforms for DBAs across the globe. Take your database administration skills to the next level by enrolling into your first course.

Follow us on Social Media:

Facebook: https://www.facebook.com/dbagenesis/
Instagram: https://www.instagram.com/dbagenesis/
Twitter: https://twitter.com/DbaGenesis
Website: https://dbagenesis.com/

All the best and goodbye for now!

Arun Kumar

Notes

www.ingramcontent.com/pod-product-compliance
Lightning Source LLC
Chambersburg PA
CBHW071254050326
40690CB00011B/2399
* 9 7 9 8 3 3 6 5 3 4 4 3 6 *